Six Geese A-Laying

The Never-Ending Holiday Ducks

ROCHELLE BRANDON, MD

© **Copyright 2024 - All rights reserved.**

The content contained within this book may not be reproduced, duplicated or transmitted without direct written permission from the author or the publisher.

Under no circumstances will any blame or legal responsibility be held against the publisher, or author, for any damages, reparation, or monetary loss due to the information contained within this book, either directly or indirectly.

Legal Notice:

This book is copyright protected. It is only for personal use. You cannot amend, distribute, sell, use, quote or paraphrase any part, or the content within this book, without the consent of the author or publisher.

Disclaimer Notice:

Please note the information contained within this document is for educational and entertainment purposes only. All effort has been executed to present accurate, up to date, reliable, complete information. No warranties of any kind are declared or implied. Readers acknowledge that the author is not engaged in the rendering of legal, financial, medical or professional advice. The content within this book has been derived from various sources. Please consult a licensed professional before attempting any techniques outlined in this book.

By reading this document, the reader agrees that under no circumstances is the author responsible for any losses, direct or indirect, that are incurred as a result of the use of the information contained within this document, including, but not limited to, errors, omissions, or inaccuracies.

About the Author

Rochelle Brandon, MD is a seasoned gynecologist with extensive experience in counseling women about the stresses of life's non-essential distractions. Having faced her own struggles with the overwhelming minutiae that can consume daily life, Dr. Brandon combines her personal experiences with professional insights to address the common, yet often overlooked, challenges that many women face. In Pecked to Death by Ducks, she shares practical advice and compassionate guidance, offering readers a roadmap to reclaim their focus and well-being amidst the chaos of modern life.

Now Dr. Brandon tackles holiday stress in Six Geese A-Laying: The Never Ending Holiday Ducks

Find out more at www.RochelleBrandon.com

Table Of Contents

Introduction: Welcome to the Holiday Duck Parade **9**

    The Mental Load of the Holiday Season 10

    The Pecking Begins: How Minor Details Add Up 12

    Setting the Tone: Humor and Practicality 13

    What You Can Expect From This Book 14

Chapter 1: The Quack of Holiday Chaos **15**

    The Holiday Duck Parade Begins:
Gift Shopping, Family Gatherings,
and Meal Prep 16

    The Cumulative Effect: How Small Tasks
Add Up to Big Stress 17

    The Quacking Takes Over: A Real-Life
Holiday Duck Parade 18

    Distractions Steal the Joy: The Perfect Gift
and the Ideal Christmas Card 20

    Real-Life Stories: The Quack of Holiday Chaos 21

Chapter 2: The Perfect Goose: Escaping the Perfectionism Trap **25**

    The Pressure to Create a Perfect Holiday 26

    The Perfectionism-Burnout Cycle 27

Recognizing When Perfectionism
Is Taking Over 29

Letting Go of Unattainable Standards 30

Combating the Perfectionism Impulse with
Mindfulness 33

Conclusion: The Freedom of Letting Go 34

Chapter 3: The Honking of Expectations: Saying No with Grace 35

The Pressure to Say Yes 36

Setting Healthy Boundaries: Why Saying No Is
Important.. 37

How to Say No Graciously 38

Real-Life Stories: Saying No with Grace 40

Reclaiming Your Holiday with Grace..................... 43

Chapter 4: Let the Ducks Waddle: Prioritizing What Matters for an Authentic Holiday 45

Urgent vs. Important: Choosing What
Matters in an Authentic Holiday 46

Moving From a Programmed to an Authentic Holiday
Experience.. 48

The Freedom of Letting Go: Let the Ducks Waddle 53

Chapter 5: The Power of Pausing: Mindfulness Amid the Noise 55

Embracing the Rhythm of the Season 56

The Importance of Sunlight and Rest................... 57

Mindfulness and Stress: Slowing Down
Amid the Noise.. 58

Table Of Contents

Practical Mindfulness Techniques
for the Holidays 59

Enhancing Holiday Moments With Mindfulness 62

Simple Mindfulness Exercises for a
Busy Schedule 63

Conclusion: Pausing to Honor the Season 64

**Chapter 6: Breaking the Holiday Duck Cycle:
How to Create Balance 65**

Rethinking Balance: It's About Energy,
Not Time 66

Strategies for Balancing Obligations and Joy 68

Practical Tips for Time Management and
Energy Preservation 70

Conclusion: Finding Your Holiday Balance 72

**Chapter 7: Don't Feed the Ducks: Protecting Your
Mental Health 75**

How Holiday Stress Impacts Mental Health 76

Recognizing the Signs of Overwhelm
and Burnout 78

Techniques for Protecting Your Mental Health 79

Cultivating a Supportive Environment 82

Conclusion: Nurturing Your Mental Health
During the Holidays 84

**Chapter 8: Tending to Your Own Nest: Self-Care
During the Holidays 85**

The Importance of Self-Care During the Holidays .. 86

Self-Care Is Essential, Not Indulgent 87

Simple Daily Self-Care Rituals 88

Restorative Self-Care Practices 90

Integrating Self-Care into Your
Holiday Routine 93

Conclusion: Self-Care as a Foundation
for Thriving.. 95

**Chapter 9: Letting the Ducks Go: Moving
Beyond the Holidays................................... 97**

Post-Holiday Reflection: Learning From
the Season 98

Letting Go Year-Round: Carrying the Holiday
Mindset Forward 100

Setting Realistic Goals for the New Year............. 101

Moving Beyond the Holidays: Embracing
Balance and Joy 104

Conclusion: Letting the Ducks Go..................... 104

**Chapter 10: Navigating Difficult Holiday
Conversations and Family Strife 107**

The Impact of Political Conversations
on Holiday Gatherings 108

Strategies for Navigating Difficult
Conversations 109

Handling Family Strife Beyond Politics................ 112

Final Thoughts: Protecting the Peace
of the Holidays 114

**Chapter 11: Embracing Imperfection:
The Beauty of a Messy Holiday 117**

The Myth of the Perfect Holiday 118

Table Of Contents

    The Beauty of Imperfection 119

    Embracing Your Version of the Holidays 121

    Final Words of Encouragement: Ducks and All 123

Chapter 12: Flying Free from the Holiday Flock 125

    Key Messages: Focus on What Truly Matters 126

    Setting Healthy, Sustainable Traditions 128

    A Final Call: Letting Go of the Ducks for Good 130

About the Author 131

Appendix 133

Recommended Reading 141

References 143

    Song References 144

Introduction

Welcome to the Holiday Duck Parade

*On the sixth day of Christmas,
my true love gave to me,
six geese a-laying.*
(Traditional, n.d.)

The holiday season—sparkling lights, the scent of pine, the joy of family togetherness. It sounds magical, right? But for many women, the reality of the holidays is far from the idyllic scenes on greeting cards. Instead, it's more like a chaotic, never-ending duck parade. A collection of annoying, quacking ducks—the kind that constantly nibble at your peace of mind, pulling you in a hundred different directions at once. These ducks represent the small, incessant distractions that seem insignificant on their own, but together, they add up to serious stress. And let's face it, they can completely derail your holiday joy.

You know these "ducks." They are the endless tasks, decisions, and expectations that pile up during the most wonderful time of the year: picking the perfect gifts, planning elaborate meals, managing holiday parties, and, of course, making sure your home looks like something out of a winter wonderland magazine. These tiny details seem minor—after all, they're just ducks!—but taken together, they can overwhelm you to the point where you're just trying to survive the holidays, not enjoy them.

In this book, we're going to confront those holiday ducks head-on. You'll learn how to recognize the ways these seemingly minor details are pecking away at your mental and emotional energy, and we'll explore strategies to help you manage them so you can reclaim your holiday joy. But before we dive into solutions, let's take a moment to acknowledge the enormous mental load women carry during the holiday season.

The Mental Load of the Holiday Season

For many women, the holiday season brings not just joy and celebration, but a hefty mental and emotional burden. You're expected to balance work, family, faith, and social obligations, all while creating magical holiday experiences for your loved ones. The reality is, the mental load of the holidays is often invisible, but it's deeply felt. It's the weight of managing the gift lists, remembering everyone's favorite dish for Christmas dinner, making sure the house is ready for guests, and, on top of all that, attending to your regular daily responsibilities.

Does that sound familiar? If you're nodding along, you're definitely not the only one. The pressure to make the holidays "perfect" can feel overwhelming. This is where our metaphorical ducks come in: They may be small, but when they swarm, they're impossible to ignore. These ducks represent all the things that seem trivial on their own, but together, they can take over your life, leaving you exhausted, frustrated, and unable to enjoy the season.

In her book *Pecked to Death by Ducks*, Dr. Rochelle Brandon explores the idea that life's minutiae—those little tasks and responsibilities—can distract us from what's profoundly important. And nowhere is this truer than during the holidays. You start with good intentions, aiming to create wonderful memories for your family, but before you know it, you're buried under a mountain of obligations. And all of those minute details, those ducks, start to steal your time and energy, leaving you feeling more stressed than joyful.

Let's break down how these ducks show up during the holidays.

- **Gift Shopping:** Finding the perfect present for everyone on your list can become an all-consuming task. Should you buy Aunt Sandra a scarf or a candle? Will your kids be disappointed if they don't get the hottest newest video game? And don't forget your coworkers, your children's teachers, and that Secret Santa exchange you didn't ask to be part of.

- **Meal Planning:** Whether you're hosting the holiday dinner or bringing a dish to someone else's home, meal planning can turn into a logistical nightmare. Is everyone on a different diet this year? Does your holiday spread need to accommodate gluten-free, dairy-free, vegan, and keto all at once?

- **Decorating:** The pressure to create a picture-perfect home can be overwhelming. From stringing up lights to setting up the tree to making sure your living room looks Instagram-ready, the decorations are another duck vying for your attention.

- **Social Expectations:** Whether it's attending holiday parties, coordinating family get-togethers, or being available for holiday traditions, the social obligations pile up quickly. And with them comes the added stress of trying to keep everyone happy.

- **Faith Responsibilities:** The holidays revolve around faith traditions of love, hope, gratitude, and relief of the poor. But all this has to be organized and managed. Often that involves children's Christmas pageants, holiday music programs, and preparing food baskets for the poor, adding to the long holiday to-do list. All of this is critically important, of course. It would not be the holiday without... Wait, do you hear quacking?

Now, none of these things on their own seem that bad, right? But together, they become a parade of holiday ducks—each one pulling you in a different direction, making it harder and harder to focus on what's profoundly important: celebrating the holidays with the people you care about.

The Pecking Begins: How Minor Details Add Up

One of the biggest challenges with holiday stress is that the things causing it often seem insignificant on their own. After all, what's one more errand or one more batch of cookies? But as Dr. Brandon highlights in *Pecked to Death by Ducks*, it's precisely this accumulation of small, seemingly unimportant tasks that lead to major stress. One little peck is kinda cute, no big deal. But numerous pecks are an attack, and all of a sudden, those cute little ducklings are a menacing collection of ducks. Each little duck is just a minor nuisance, but when there are dozens of them all demanding your attention, they can leave you feeling like you're being nibbled to death.

This kind of stress doesn't just drain your energy—it also robs you of the ability to fully engage with the things that matter most. When you're so focused on keeping up with the minutiae of the holidays, it's hard to find the time or mental space to genuinely enjoy the season. You might miss special moments with your family or find yourself snapping at loved ones because you're so overwhelmed by your never-ending to-do list. This is where we need to hit pause and recognize that all of these ducks are distractions, pulling us away from the joy and connection that make the holidays special.

Setting the Tone: Humor and Practicality

Now, if all this talk of holiday stress is making you feel even more overwhelmed, take a deep breath. The goal of this book isn't to add more pressure or give you a whole new list of things to do. Quite the opposite. This book is about giving you permission to let go of some of those ducks, to focus on what truly matters, and to laugh at the absurdity of it all along the way.

Because let's face it: The holiday season can be ridiculous. The pressure to make everything perfect, the endless parade of events, the expectation that we'll all somehow emerge in January feeling refreshed and renewed—sometimes, the best way to deal with the madness is to embrace it with a sense of humor. We're going to tackle the holiday ducks with both humor and practicality so you can find a balance between the chaos and the joy.

What You Can Expect From This Book

Throughout this book, we'll explore a mix of mindset shifts, actionable strategies, and lighthearted survival tactics to help you reclaim your holiday season. Here's a sneak peek of what's coming:

- **Mindset Shifts:** We'll work on shifting your perspective from "everything has to be perfect" to "good enough is more than enough." You'll learn how to let go of perfectionism and embrace a more relaxed, joyful approach to the holidays.

- **Actionable Strategies:** We'll dive into practical tips for managing the holiday chaos, from setting boundaries with family and friends to streamlining your holiday to-do list. You'll learn how to prioritize what matters most and let go of the rest.

- **Lighthearted Tactics:** Humor is going to be our secret weapon. We'll explore how to laugh at the inevitable holiday mishaps and find joy in the imperfections. After all, the best memories often come from the things that didn't go according to plan.

By the end of this book, you'll feel more empowered to enjoy the holidays on your terms, free from the constant pecking of minor details and distractions. Together, we'll figure out how to let the ducks waddle by without letting them take over your life.

So grab a cup of cocoa (or maybe something stronger), sit back, and let's get ready to tackle those holiday ducks one quack at a time.

Chapter 1

The Quack of Holiday Chaos

*I heard the bells on Christmas day
Their old familiar carols play
And mild and sweet their songs repeat
Of peace on Earth, good will to men.*
(Longfellow, 1863)

It's that time of year again—decorations are up, the malls are packed, and your to-do list is growing longer by the day. The holiday season has officially begun. What's supposed to be a joyful time of celebration and connection often turns into a frantic race to the finish line filled with endless shopping, cooking, family gatherings, and parties. For many women, it feels like a chaotic whirlwind where each day brings more demands, more expectations, and more stress.

As you navigate the holiday season, you may find yourself juggling everything from gift shopping to meal preparation, from hosting relatives to attending holiday events. These tasks, while seemingly small in isolation, add up quickly, creating a level of chaos that can leave you feeling overwhelmed. This is where the "quacking" begins—the constant noise of minor tasks that can distract you from the bigger picture of what the holidays are really about: joy, connection, and meaning.

The Holiday Duck Parade Begins: Gift Shopping, Family Gatherings, and Meal Prep

Let's start with one of the biggest holiday stressors: *gift shopping*. Finding the perfect present for everyone on your list can quickly become an all-consuming task. It starts with the best intentions: You want to give meaningful, thoughtful gifts to the people you love. But somewhere between battling the crowds at the mall and scouring online stores for that one specific item, the pressure mounts. What was supposed to be a fun and generous gesture turns into a frantic scavenger hunt. And, of course, finding the perfect gift on a budget is nigh impossible, adding an additional layer of stress. Is this toy good enough for my niece? Will my mother-in-law actually use this kitchen gadget? Should I add a personal touch with custom wrapping paper or hand-written notes? Before you know it, your mind is spinning, consumed by the details of gift-giving.

Then, of course, there's the *family gatherings*. Whether you're hosting a holiday dinner or attending one at a relative's house, family events are a staple of the season. But they can also be a source of stress. You might find yourself worrying about whether everyone will get along, whether you've made enough food, or whether your home looks "holiday ready." Family dynamics often come with their own set of expectations, and the pressure to make everything perfect can weigh heavily on your shoulders. And as if we don't have enough going on during the holidays, some years we have major elections inciting politically charged family arguments... uhm... I mean discussions.

And let's not forget *meal prep*. Planning, shopping for, and cooking a holiday feast is no small feat. Do I need to prepare an entirely separate meal for the gluten-free cousin and the keto aunt? Whether it's Christmas dinner, Kwanzaa, Hanukkah celebrations, or any other holiday gathering, the pressure to provide a memorable meal is enormous. The turkey needs to be perfectly roasted, the side dishes timed just right, and the dessert must impress. You're juggling oven space, keeping an eye on the clock, and trying to keep your cool while Aunt Goose critiques your gravy.

In my family, we have fried turkey. You have not lived until you are hosting the whole family, and you have a seasoned, brined *raw* turkey four hours before dinner. I have never prayed so hard as when I baptized that turkey in boiling oil. You can imagine my shouts of hallelujah for the Christmas miracle when that bird was done, crisp, juicy, and golden right in time for dinner. All of these tasks may seem small in isolation, but taken together, they become a tidal wave of anxiety and responsibilities.

The Cumulative Effect: How Small Tasks Add Up to Big Stress

The challenge with these holiday tasks is that they seem minor on their own. Buying one gift, cooking one meal, attending one party—it all sounds manageable. But what makes the holiday season so stressful is the accumulation of these tasks. Each individual responsibility may not seem like a big deal, but when they pile up, they can become overwhelming.

This is where the "quacking" comes in—the endless noise of small, incessant tasks that demand your attention. As each new responsibility pops up, it distracts you from what really matters. Instead of focusing on the joy of the season, you find yourself mentally drained from managing a thousand tiny details. It's as though you're being pecked at by a gaggle of geese, each one nibbling away at your energy and attention.

Take *decorating*, for example. Decorating your home for the holidays can be a fun and festive activity, but it's easy to get caught up in the details. Do the lights on the tree match the ones outside? Is the wreath on the front door big enough? Should you add more tinsel, or is it too much? Before long, you're obsessing over every inch of your home, trying to create a picture-perfect holiday scene. The decorations, which should bring joy, have instead become another source of stress.

These seemingly small, everyday tasks slowly accumulate until they take up so much of your mental bandwidth that there's little room left for anything else. You start to lose sight of why you're doing all of this in the first place—to celebrate, to practice your faith, to connect, to create memories with the people you love.

The Quacking Takes Over: A Real-Life Holiday Duck Parade

Let me set the scene. It's a crisp December afternoon in Charlotte, and I'm rushing around, trying to finish my last-minute errands. You know the kind—those final, frantic dashes to pick up wrapping paper, last-minute gifts, or ingredients for the big meal. I was already stressed out, juggling a mental list of everything I still needed to do, when I got stuck in the middle of holiday traffic. If you've ever driven in Charlotte during the holidays, you know that the roads can feel like a NASCAR race. I'm on Mallard Creek Road—yes, *Mallard Creek Road*—when suddenly, traffic grinds to a complete halt. I thought it was a car accident. After a few minutes of bumper-to-bumper standstill, the cars ahead start moving again, and I see the real culprits: a collection of Mallard ducks with ducklings, proudly and methodically marching across all four lanes as if they own the place.

Now, these weren't your typical holiday birds—they weren't turkeys or even the proverbial Christmas goose. These were ducks with a mission, and that mission was to remind us all just how little control we actually have over the holiday madness. Here we were, a bunch of harried humans, stopped dead in our tracks by a bunch of determined waterfowl. And the best part? The notoriously impatient drivers around me—who usually approach speed limits like mere suggestions—actually waited. No honking, no swerving, just a collective pause to let these ducks take their sweet time. And the ducks were just waddling along, oblivious to the chaos around them.

As I sat there watching these ducks waddle their way to wherever ducks go, I couldn't help but laugh at the absurdity of it all. I also couldn't help but think about how perfectly this moment encapsulated the essence of the holiday season—one part joy, two parts chaos, with a dash of unexpected surprises. Sometimes, ducks really can be a good thing. And no, not just with mint sauce.

Once the ducks safely made it to the other side, the race resumed—drivers zoomed off, and I went back to my errands. But that brief encounter with those holiday ducks stayed with me. It was a reminder that sometimes, we need to let go of the hustle and just enjoy the moment, even if it's forced upon us by a parade of actual ducks.

Distractions Steal the Joy: The Perfect Gift and the Ideal Christmas Card

One of the biggest holiday stressors is the pursuit of perfection. We're often chasing the idea of the "perfect" holiday—the perfect meal, the perfect decorations, the perfect gift. But this pursuit can consume so much of our mental energy that we lose sight of what's really important.

Take the example of finding the *perfect gift*. It's easy to get caught up in the idea that you need to buy something special for everyone on your list. You spend hours online comparing prices, reading reviews, and second-guessing your choices. What if they don't like it? What if it's not personal enough? Before long, what should be a thoughtful gesture becomes a source of anxiety. The pressure to get it right can be overwhelming, and instead of feeling excited about giving, you're stressed about whether you've done enough.

Then there's the *Christmas card*—the hallmark of holiday perfection. Whether it's picking out the right design or planning the perfect family photo, the pressure to send out an ideal holiday card can be intense. Maybe you're debating whether to go for a funny card, a classic one, or something that perfectly captures your family's holiday spirit. You spend hours coordinating outfits for the family photo only for the kids to melt down during the photo shoot or for your dog to refuse to cooperate. The result? Another source of holiday stress, all for the sake of creating a flawless holiday moment.

But here's the thing: The perfect gift, the perfect card, the perfect anything isn't what makes the holidays meaningful. In fact, the pursuit of perfection can often distract you from the very things that matter most—connection, love, and shared experiences.

Real-Life Stories: The Quack of Holiday Chaos

I'm not alone in feeling the pressure of holiday chaos. Women everywhere can relate to the stress of managing a million small tasks during the holiday season. Here are a few real-life stories from women who, like me, have been pecked to death by holiday ducks:

- **Jasmine's Christmas Crisis:** Jasmine, a mother of two, spent weeks preparing for the holidays. She meticulously planned her family's Christmas Eve dinner down to the smallest detail. But when the big day arrived, her oven broke down, leaving her with a half-cooked turkey and a house full of hungry guests. "I was so stressed about making everything perfect that I didn't even enjoy the day," she said. "Looking back, I wish I'd just let go of some of those little details and focused on spending time with my family."

- **Piper's Gift-Giving Gauntlet:** Piper found herself caught up in the pressure to find the perfect gift for everyone on her list. She spent hours searching online, driving to different stores, and comparing options. "I wanted to get something special for each person, but I ended up feeling completely overwhelmed," she said. "By the time Christmas morning came, I was exhausted, and I didn't even enjoy watching people open their gifts because I was so worried about whether they liked them."

- **Nala's Decorating Disaster:** Nala loves decorating for the holidays, but last year, she found herself going overboard. "I spent so much time trying to make every corner of my house look perfect," she said. "I wanted everything to be Instagram-worthy, but in the end, I realized I was doing it for other people, not for myself. I was so stressed about the decorations that I didn't even get to relax and enjoy the holidays."

These stories aren't unique—they're experiences that many women can relate to. The holiday season, with all its joy and beauty, can also bring a lot of pressure, and it's easy to get caught up in the quack of holiday chaos. But the good news is, there's a way to manage it. You can learn to quiet the quacking and focus on what really matters.

In the next chapter, we'll explore how perfectionism—one of the biggest holiday ducks—can take over and what you can do to free yourself from its grip. Because while we may not be able to avoid the holiday chaos entirely, we can learn to manage it in a way that lets us find peace and joy amid the noise.

The Quack of Holiday Chaos

Chapter 2

The Perfect Goose: Escaping the Perfectionism Trap

*Jesu, joy of man's desiring,
Holy wisdom, love most bright;
Drawn by Thee, our souls aspiring
Soar to uncreated light.*
(Bach, 1723)

For many women, the holidays are not just a time for celebration—they're also an opportunity to create magical, picture-perfect experiences for their families. From decorating the house to preparing holiday meals, from selecting thoughtful gifts to orchestrating joyful gatherings, there's an unspoken pressure to make everything perfect. And while the intention behind this effort is noble—after all, who doesn't want to create a warm and festive atmosphere?—the relentless pursuit of perfection often comes at a steep cost.

During the holidays, perfectionism can quickly become magnified. The desire to deliver flawless experiences for your loved ones can lead to exhaustion, burnout, and a sense of never quite measuring up. Instead of savoring the joy of the season, you may find yourself caught in a spiral of stress, anxiety, and overwhelm, trying to meet standards that are not only unattainable but also unnecessary. In this chapter, we'll explore how perfectionism manifests during the holidays, why it's so damaging, and how you can break free from its grip to reclaim a more joyful, balanced holiday experience.

The Pressure to Create a Perfect Holiday

It's no secret that women often bear the emotional and logistical burden of holiday planning. Whether it's preparing the perfect meal, coordinating family schedules, or making sure the holiday cards get mailed on time, there's a sense of responsibility that falls heavily on women's shoulders. And while many women take pride in making the holidays special for their families, this pressure can quickly snowball into the expectation that everything must be flawless.

Perfectionism during the holidays shows up in many forms:

- **The Perfect Meal:** The pressure to prepare an elaborate, multicourse feast that impresses everyone at the table. Every dish must be timed perfectly, every recipe must be executed without a hitch, and every dietary preference must be accommodated.

- **The Perfect Home:** The desire to transform your home into a holiday wonderland, where every decoration is artfully arranged, every light is twinkling just right, and every room is Instagram-worthy.

- **The Perfect Gifts:** The pursuit of finding the ideal present for each person on your list. It's not just about giving a gift—it's about giving something that's thoughtful, unique, and perfectly suited to the recipient's tastes and needs.
- **The Perfect Gathering:** Hosting a holiday event that runs seamlessly, where everyone is happy, entertained, and grateful. The food is delicious, the house is spotless, and the conversation flows effortlessly.

These expectations may sound familiar, and on the surface, they might seem reasonable. After all, who doesn't want to make their holiday celebrations memorable and enjoyable? But the problem with perfectionism is that it rarely stops at "good enough." Instead, it demands that every detail be executed flawlessly, leaving little room for flexibility, spontaneity, or even mistakes. And when perfection becomes the goal, the joy of the season can quickly be replaced by stress, frustration, and a sense of inadequacy.

The Perfectionism-Burnout Cycle

One of the most insidious aspects of perfectionism is the way it leads to burnout. The pursuit of perfection requires an immense amount of time, energy, and mental focus—resources that are already in short supply during the busy holiday season. As you strive to meet impossible standards, you may find yourself feeling overwhelmed, exhausted, and emotionally drained. Here's how the perfectionism-burnout cycle typically unfolds:

1. **The Ambitious Start:** At the beginning of the holiday season, you may feel excited and

energized. You set ambitious goals for yourself—perhaps you plan an elaborate holiday dinner, decide to hand-make personalized gifts, or aim to host a picture-perfect family gathering. At this stage, your enthusiasm drives you to take on more and more tasks.

2. **The Mid-Season Overload:** As the holidays approach, the sheer volume of tasks begins to weigh you down. You may find yourself spending hours decorating the house, redoing a batch of cookies that didn't turn out quite right, or scouring stores for the perfect gift. The pressure to keep up with your exacting standards grows, and you start to feel the strain.

3. **The Burnout Phase:** By the time the holidays are in full swing, you're running on empty. You're physically exhausted from all the cooking, cleaning, shopping, and socializing. Mentally, you're drained from trying to keep everything "just right." Emotionally, you may feel disappointed or frustrated that things aren't turning out exactly as you envisioned. At this point, the joy and excitement you initially felt have been replaced by stress and fatigue.

4. **The Post-Holiday Collapse:** After the holidays, you may feel completely burned out. Instead of feeling fulfilled by your efforts, you may experience a sense of emptiness or even regret. You spent so much time chasing perfection that you missed the simple pleasures of the season—spending time with loved ones, enjoying a cozy night by the fire, or just relaxing.

The perfectionism-burnout cycle is exhausting, and yet many women fall into it year after year. The good news is, there's a way to break free from this cycle and create a holiday experience that's joyful, fulfilling, and—most importantly—sustainable.

Recognizing When Perfectionism Is Taking Over

One of the first steps in escaping the perfectionism trap is learning to recognize when it's taking over. Perfectionism often sneaks up on us, disguised as a desire to "do our best" or "go the extra mile." But there's a fine line between putting in a good effort and driving ourselves to the point of exhaustion. Here are some signs that perfectionism might be creeping in during the holidays:

- **You're Constantly Revising and Tweaking:** Whether it's the holiday menu, the decorations, or the seating arrangement for a family gathering, you find yourself revisiting decisions repeatedly, trying to make everything just a little bit better. This constant tweaking can be a sign that you're aiming for perfection rather than simply enjoying the process.

- **You're Comparing Yourself to Others:** Social media, family traditions, and even childhood memories can create a sense of comparison. You might feel pressure to recreate the "perfect" holiday moments you see online or remember from years past. If you find yourself constantly measuring your holiday efforts against others, perfectionism is likely at play.

- **You're Saying "Yes" to Everything:** Perfectionists often struggle with setting boundaries. You may feel compelled to say "yes" to every invitation, volunteer for every school event, or take on extra tasks to ensure everything goes smoothly. If you're overcommitted and feeling stretched too thin, it's time to reevaluate.
- **You're Focusing on Details at the Expense of the Big Picture:** Perfectionism tends to zero in on the minutiae. Maybe you're obsessing over finding the right shade of ribbon for your gift wrapping or spending hours trying to get your Christmas tree lights exactly right. While these details can be fun, if they're causing you stress and taking time away from more meaningful activities, perfectionism is in control.

Letting Go of Unattainable Standards

Once you've recognized that perfectionism is taking over, the next step is to actively let go of unattainable standards. This doesn't mean lowering your expectations or abandoning your desire to create a beautiful holiday experience. Instead, it means shifting your focus from perfection to authenticity, from "doing it all" to doing what truly matters. Here are some strategies to help you let go of the perfectionism trap.

Embrace the Concept of "Good Enough"

One of the most powerful ways to escape perfectionism is to adopt a mindset of "good enough." This doesn't mean settling for mediocrity or cutting corners—it means recognizing that what you're doing is already enough. Whether it's your holiday meal, your decorations, or your gift choices, trust that your effort is enough to create a meaningful experience. The holidays aren't about impressing others—they're about spending time with the people you care about.

Try asking yourself, *"Will this really matter a year from now?"* Will anyone remember whether the table settings matched or whether the dessert was homemade? Chances are the answer is no. What people will remember is how they felt—whether they felt loved, welcomed, and included.

Prioritize What Truly Matters

During the holidays, it's easy to get inundated with the tsunami of tasks and activities. To combat perfectionism, it's important to take a step back and identify what truly matters to you. Is it spending time with family? Is it creating a sense of warmth and connection in your home? Is it honoring a meaningful tradition?

Once you've identified your priorities, focus your energy on those things, and let go of the rest. Maybe that means skipping the elaborate gift wrapping in favor of spending more time with your kids. Maybe it means simplifying your holiday menu so you can enjoy more time around the dinner table. By focusing on what truly matters, you'll free yourself from the pressure to do it all.

Set Realistic Expectations

Perfectionism often comes from setting unrealistic expectations—for yourself, for others, and for the holiday season itself. Take a moment to check in with your expectations. Are they reasonable, or are you setting yourself up for disappointment?

If you're hosting a holiday gathering, for example, expect that not everything will go according to plan. Maybe the turkey will take longer to cook than expected, or maybe a guest will spill wine on the tablecloth. These things happen, and they don't have to ruin the celebration. In fact, embracing imperfections can lead to some of the most memorable and lighthearted moments.

I often find myself pecked by the perfectionist duck around the holidays, striving to recreate the joy of my childhood Christmases. For years, I believed that joy came from the food, the decorations, the gifts, and all the "stuff" that I now associate with holiday magic. But after many seasons of chasing that elusive feeling only to end up stressed and overwhelmed, I decided to replay those childhood memories in my mind. What I realized was that, as a child, the holidays were so joyous not because of the food or the presents, but because I had no responsibilities. My parents shielded me from the stresses of holiday preparations, allowing me to bask in the simple joy of being with family. The laughter, the stories from my grandparents, the playful teasing, and the warmth of togetherness were the real magic.

My parents, on the other hand, carried the weight of holiday travel costs, the pressure of gift-giving, and the stress of making it all happen. They weren't perfect holidays—they were messy and real, but I was blissfully unaware of that. With this realization, I knew I had to let go of the illusion that holiday joy comes from perfectly orchestrating every detail. Instead, it's about the connections we share and the moments of laughter and love. I want the children in my family to remember the holidays the same way I did—filled with joy, not because everything was perfect, but because we were together. And I certainly don't want them to remember me as a frazzled, overwhelmed Auntie but as someone who was fully present, enjoying the beauty of the moment.

Combating the Perfectionism Impulse with Mindfulness

Mindfulness is one of the most effective tools for managing perfectionism. By practicing mindfulness, you can cultivate awareness of your thoughts, emotions, and behaviors, allowing you to notice when perfectionism is creeping in and choose a more balanced approach. Here are some mindfulness techniques to help you combat the perfectionism impulse during the holidays:

The "Pause and Breathe" Technique

When you feel yourself getting caught up in the holiday rush—whether it's stressing over the menu or trying to perfect the gift wrapping—take a moment to pause and breathe. This simple act of pausing helps break the cycle of frantic perfectionism and allows you to step back from the situation. As you breathe, ask yourself, *"What's most important right now?"* This question can help you refocus on what truly matters.

Practice Gratitude

Perfectionism thrives on dissatisfaction—on the belief that things aren't quite good enough. To counter this, practice gratitude. Take a moment each day to reflect on what's going well, what you're thankful for, and what you've already accomplished. Gratitude helps shift your mindset from "not enough" to "more than enough," reminding you that the holiday season is full of blessings, even if it's not perfect.

Mindful Acceptance

Mindful acceptance is about embracing the reality of the present moment, imperfections and all. If something doesn't go according to plan—a recipe fails, a gift is late, or a decoration doesn't turn out the way you imagined—practice accepting it without judgment. Remind yourself that the holidays aren't about perfection—they're about presence. By accepting the imperfections, you create space for more joy, connection, and peace.

Conclusion: The Freedom of Letting Go

The holidays can be a time of incredible joy, but they can also be a breeding ground for perfectionism. By recognizing when perfectionism is taking over and consciously letting go of unattainable standards, you can break free from the stress and burnout that often accompany the season. Instead of striving for the perfect goose, focus on what truly matters—connection, love, and shared experiences. With mindfulness and a willingness to embrace imperfection, you can create a holiday season that's not only good enough, but deeply fulfilling.

Chapter 3

The Honking of Expectations: Saying No with Grace

*Don we now our gay apparel,
Fa la la la la, la la la la
Troll the ancient Yuletide carol,
Fa la la la la, la la la la.*
Deck the Halls (Traditional, n.d.)

The holidays are often described as the season of giving—giving gifts, giving time, giving love. But for many women, the holidays are also the season of *giving in* to social and familial expectations. We're expected to say yes to every event, tradition, and request that comes our way, often at the expense of our own time, energy, and well-being. The result? Instead of feeling the joy and connection the holidays promise, we feel overwhelmed, exhausted, and sometimes resentful.

Whether it's family gatherings, work parties, or social obligations, the honking of holiday expectations can be deafening. Everyone seems to want a piece of you—your time, your energy, your attention—and it's easy to fall into the trap of saying yes to everything in an effort to please others. But constantly saying yes can leave you with little room to prioritize what truly matters to you. In this chapter, we'll examine how holiday expectations can add pressure, explore the importance of setting healthy boundaries, and offer practical strategies for saying "no" graciously—without the guilt.

The Pressure to Say Yes

There's a certain cultural narrative around the holidays that glorifies being busy. We're encouraged to participate in every activity, attend every event, and uphold every tradition, all while keeping a smile on our faces and making everything look effortless. For women, the pressure to say yes can be particularly intense. Society often places women in the roles of nurturer and caretaker, and the holidays magnify these expectations. Whether it's volunteering at school, hosting family dinners, or organizing office parties, women are frequently expected to step up and make the holidays special for everyone around them.

The problem with this expectation is that it doesn't leave much room for our own needs. Instead of enjoying the holidays, you may find yourself running from one obligation to the next, trying to keep up with a never-ending list of commitments. Over time, this can lead to burnout, frustration, and a sense of losing control over your own holiday experience.

Here are a few examples of how holiday expectations can pile up:

- **Family Gatherings:** Maybe your family expects you to host Thanksgiving every year, or perhaps your in-laws assume you'll attend every holiday event they plan, no matter how far the drive or how inconvenient the timing. And everyone wants to see the grandkids this holiday. How can you say no?

- **Social Events:** Between work holiday parties, gatherings with friends, and community events, your calendar can quickly fill up. It's easy to feel obligated to attend every event you're invited to, even if it means sacrificing your own downtime.

- **Traditions:** Whether it's decorating the house, baking cookies, or attending holiday services, family traditions can carry a lot of weight. You might feel pressure to keep every tradition alive, even if it's not something you enjoy or have time for. I have a friend who resents that elf on the shelf. "It's just one more expectation to uphold every year!" she says.

While these activities can be fun and meaningful, the sheer volume of them can be overwhelming. And when you feel like you *have* to say yes to everything, it's easy to lose sight of your own needs and values.

Setting Healthy Boundaries: Why Saying No Is Important

The first step to reclaiming your time and energy during the holidays is recognizing that it's okay to say no. In fact, saying no is an essential part of maintaining healthy boundaries. When you set boundaries, you're protecting your time, your energy, and your mental health. You're giving yourself permission to prioritize what matters most to you, rather than trying to meet everyone else's expectations.

For many women, the idea of saying no can feel uncomfortable or even guilt-inducing. You might worry that by saying no, you're letting someone down or that you'll be judged as selfish or ungrateful. But the truth is, setting boundaries protects your peace of mind. It's about recognizing your limits and understanding that you can't be everything to everyone. By saying no when you need to, you're not only taking care of yourself—you're also ensuring that the things you do say yes to receive your full attention and energy.

Here's why saying no is important during the holiday season:

- **Prevents Burnout:** Constantly saying yes can leave you feeling drained and depleted. By setting boundaries, you give yourself the space to recharge and enjoy the activities that truly matter to you.

- **Creates More Meaningful Connections***:* When you're overcommitted, it's hard to be fully present with the people you care about. By saying no to some obligations, you create more time and energy to connect meaningfully with your loved ones.

- **Protects Your Peace of Mind:** The holidays should be a time of joy and reflection, but when you're overwhelmed by commitments, it's hard to find that peace. Setting boundaries allows you to protect your mental and emotional well-being.

How to Say No Graciously

Saying no doesn't have to be harsh or confrontational. In fact, with a little thoughtfulness and grace, you can decline invitations and requests in a way that preserves your relationships and maintains your peace of mind. The key is to be clear, honest, and kind. Here are some strategies for saying no without guilt:

Be Honest and Direct

When you say no, it's important to be clear and direct about your decision. Avoid giving vague responses like "maybe" or "I'll think about it" if you know you're not able to commit. Being honest from the start helps prevent misunderstandings and shows that you respect both your time and the other person's.

Example:

- "I'd love to participate, but I'm already committed to several other events this season, so I won't be able to join this time."

Express Gratitude

If someone has invited you to an event or asked for your help, it's always a good idea to express gratitude before declining. This shows that you appreciate the offer, even if you're unable to accept.

Example:

- "Thank you so much for thinking of me! I really appreciate the invitation, but I'm going to have to decline this year."

Offer an Alternative

If you feel comfortable doing so, you can offer an alternative that works better for you. This could be as simple as suggesting another date for a get-together or offering to contribute in a smaller way.

Example:

- "I won't be able to attend the event, but I'd love to catch up after the holidays if you're available!"

Use the "Busy" Card

Sometimes, it's enough to simply let someone know that your schedule is already full. You don't have to explain every detail—just a simple statement that you're busy can be enough.

Example:

- "I'm really flattered that you asked, but my schedule is packed this season, so I won't be able to take on anything additional."

Prioritize Self-Care

Remember that saying no is an act of self-care. When you decline a request, you're protecting your time and energy so that you can be fully present for the things that matter most to you.

Example:

- "I've been feeling a little overwhelmed lately, so I'm trying to keep things low-key this holiday season. I hope you understand!"

Real-Life Stories: Saying No with Grace

Let's take a look at some real-life examples of women who have successfully set boundaries during the holidays and reclaimed their peace.

Aisha: Declining Multiple Roles

Aisha was deeply involved in her church community, and every year, she was asked to direct multiple holiday programs. She had a reputation for being incredibly organized and creative, so it was no surprise when she was asked to lead the children's choir, coordinate the dancing angels, and oversee the Sunday school holiday pageant—all in the same season! At first, she felt flattered and didn't want to disappoint anyone, so she agreed.

But as the holidays approached, Aisha started to feel overwhelmed. She realized that taking on all of these responsibilities was leaving her little time to enjoy the season with her own family. She knew she needed to set boundaries, but she was nervous about saying no. After some reflection, she decided to decline some of the roles, explaining that while she loved being involved, she couldn't take on all three projects this year.

Aisha's script:

- "I'm so honored that you thought of me for these roles, but I've realized that I'm overcommitted this season. I'll be happy to direct the children's choir, but I'll need to step back from the other two projects to ensure I can give my best to the choir and still enjoy time with my family."

By being honest and kind, Aisha was able to maintain her involvement without feeling overwhelmed.

Sophia: Asking for Help with Hosting

Sophia loved hosting her family for the holidays, but last year, her relatives asked if they could stay for 10 days—double the usual time. Sophia agreed, but as the days went by, she found herself stressed by the constant cooking, cleaning, and entertaining. She felt like she was spending all her time in the kitchen, and she wasn't able to relax or enjoy her family's company.

This year, Sophia decided to set a boundary. When her family asked to stay again, she welcomed them but made it clear that she needed help with meals and cleanup. Instead of feeling guilty for asking, she felt empowered to make the holiday experience more manageable for herself.

Sophia's script:

- "I'm so happy to have everyone stay again this year! To make things a little easier, I'd love it if we could share the responsibilities for meals and cleanup. How about we all pitch in and take turns so that everyone can enjoy some downtime?"

Sophia's family was more than willing to help, and the shared responsibility made the holiday much less stressful.

Lian: Saying No to Endless Holiday Parties

Lian and her husband both worked in corporate jobs, and every December, they were invited to an endless stream of holiday parties—work events, family parties, and social gatherings with friends. While they enjoyed some of the celebrations, the sheer number of invitations became overwhelming, not to mention expensive. One year, they found themselves running from one event to the next, spending more time on the road than actually enjoying the season.

The next year, Lian and her husband made the decision to say no to many of the parties. They prioritized a few events they genuinely wanted to attend and graciously declined the rest. They also opted out of several Secret Santa gift exchanges to preserve their holiday budget.

Lian's script:

- "We're really grateful for the invitation, but we've decided to keep things simple this year and focus on a few quiet evenings at home. We hope you have a wonderful time, and we look forward to catching up in the new year!"

By setting these boundaries, Lian and her husband were able to enjoy a more peaceful and intentional holiday season, free from the pressure of attending every event.

Reclaiming Your Holiday with Grace

Saying no during the holidays isn't about shutting people out—it's about creating space for the things that matter most. When you set boundaries and prioritize your own well-being, you're better able to show up fully for the people and activities that bring you joy. Remember, the holidays aren't about doing everything perfectly or pleasing everyone—they're about connection, love, and presence.

As you move forward, practice setting boundaries. It may feel uncomfortable at first, but with practice, you'll find that saying no with grace becomes easier. You'll gain confidence in your ability to protect your time and energy, and you'll experience the freedom that comes with choosing how you want to spend your holiday season.

In the next chapter, we'll explore how to prioritize what truly matters during the holidays so you can focus on creating meaningful experiences rather than getting lost in the noise of holiday demands.

Chapter 4

Let the Ducks Waddle: Prioritizing What Matters for an Authentic Holiday

*Go, tell it on the mountain,
Over the hills and everywhere
Go, tell it on the mountain.
That Jesus Christ is born.*
(Traditional, n.d.)

When we think about the holiday season, we often picture the perfect, programmed version we've been taught to strive for. It's the scene straight out of a commercial: a perfectly decorated home, a table overflowing with food, gifts stacked high under the tree, and smiling faces all around. But how often does the pressure to meet these unrealistic ideals drain us of the very joy we're seeking? Year after year, many of us run through the motions of what we've been conditioned to believe is the "right" way to celebrate the holidays—buying more, doing more, and exhausting ourselves in the process.

This chapter is about breaking free from the "programmed" holiday experience and embracing a more *authentic* one. Instead of running on autopilot—buying gifts that no one needs, stressing over hosting the perfect meal, and attending events out of obligation—we'll explore how to prioritize what truly matters. The holiday season is a time for reflection, connection, and joy, but only if we intentionally choose to focus on the things that align with our personal values.

We'll talk about shifting the tone of the holidays from one of consumption to one of deeper meaning—whether that's through creating new spiritual or religious traditions, focusing on giving back to those in need, or even letting go of the expectation that you have to host or cook for every holiday gathering. It's time to let the ducks waddle—to allow the distractions of perfection and obligation to pass by, while you reclaim the things that truly bring you joy and fulfillment.

Urgent vs. Important: Choosing What Matters in an Authentic Holiday

One of the first steps in creating an authentic holiday experience is distinguishing between what's *urgent* and what's *important*. Urgent tasks often come with a sense of immediate pressure—like last-minute shopping, holiday parties you feel obligated to attend, or cooking elaborate meals. These tasks can easily take over your holiday schedule, but they don't necessarily align with your core values.

Important tasks, on the other hand, are those that bring you closer to what truly matters. These are the experiences and connections that nourish your soul and align with your deeper sense of purpose. They may not always scream for your attention, but they hold the real meaning behind the holidays.

For example, instead of scrambling to buy the perfect gift for everyone on your list, maybe what's important to you is creating quality time with your loved ones. Maybe it is more important to take the children to visit their lonely great grandma. Instead of cooking a huge meal that leaves you exhausted, maybe the important thing is enjoying a peaceful, relaxed evening with those who matter most. It may be more important to get takeout and have a family game marathon.

The Urgent vs. Important Reflection

To help you sort through your holiday to-do list, try this simple reflection exercise:

1. **Make a List of Everything on Your Holiday Calendar:** Include all the parties, gift exchanges, traditions, meal preparations, and decorating that you're planning to do.

2. **For Each Item, Ask Yourself:**
   - Is this urgent (time-sensitive but not necessarily meaningful)?
   - Is this important (aligned with my core values and what I genuinely want out of the holiday season)?

3. **Prioritize Accordingly:** Once you've identified what's truly important, focus your energy there. Let the urgent tasks waddle by—if they don't

contribute to your sense of joy or meaning, it's okay to let them go.

We discussed the Duck Priority Matrix in my prior book, *Pecked to Death: How Minutiae Can Distract You from Living Your Best Life*.

By making this distinction, you'll be able to cut through the noise of holiday expectations and get to the heart of what matters most to you.

Moving From a Programmed to an Authentic Holiday Experience

Many of us fall into the trap of a "programmed" holiday, where we follow the script handed down by consumer culture and societal expectations. We think we have to buy more, do more, and entertain more in order to have a successful holiday. But what if we could opt out of the holiday rat race and design an experience that feels more authentic to who we are and what we value?

An authentic holiday experience doesn't have to follow the usual script. It's about stripping away the external pressures and finding deeper meaning in how you celebrate. This might mean focusing less on materialism and more on connection, or less on performing holiday duties and more on creating spiritual or reflective moments. Here are some ways to start shifting toward a more meaningful, less commercial holiday season.

Set New Traditions with a Spiritual or Reflective Focus

Instead of getting caught up in the material aspects of the holidays, consider creating new traditions that focus on spirituality or reflection. Whether you celebrate

Christmas, Hanukkah, Kwanzaa, or simply embrace the festive season, adding a reflective or spiritual element can make the holidays feel more grounded and purposeful.

- **Daily Reflection Ritual:** You might set aside a few minutes each day in December to reflect on what you're grateful for, your hopes for the new year, or the blessings you've received over the past year. Light a candle or create a peaceful space for this practice.

- **Community Giving Tradition:** Instead of focusing on receiving gifts, consider making it a family tradition to give back. This could mean volunteering at a local shelter, donating to a cause you care about, or adopting a family in need and shopping for their essentials.

- **Religious Practices:** If you come from a religious background, this is a wonderful time to reconnect with your faith traditions. Whether through prayer, attending services, or engaging in sacred rituals, centering your holidays on spirituality can bring a deeper sense of meaning.

Donate in Honor of Loved Ones Instead of Gifting

Gift-giving can feel wonderful, but let's be honest: So many of the gifts we exchange during the holidays end up forgotten, unused, or unwanted. Instead of getting caught in the frantic cycle of buying gifts just for the sake of it, consider shifting your focus toward *giving with purpose*. One meaningful way to do this is to make donations in honor of your loved ones.

Instead of a mad dash through the mall or endless scrolling through online stores, you can donate to charities or causes that reflect the values of your friends and family.

Not only does this simplify your holiday shopping, but it also contributes to something bigger than consumerism. Here are some ideas for donation-based gifting:

- **Adopt a Family:** Many organizations offer programs where you can adopt a family for the holidays, helping provide meals, clothing, and gifts for those in need. Involve your own family in shopping for the adopted family's needs and let this be a tradition rooted in giving.

- **Donate to a Meaningful Cause:** Instead of buying material gifts, consider donating to a charity that resonates with your loved one's passions—whether it's environmental conservation, education, or health-related causes. Other examples of such gifts would be planting trees in someone's name, supporting fair-trade artisans, or purchasing from companies that donate a portion of profits to charity.

- **Give Back Through Experiences:** You can also give experiential gifts that give back, such as a cooking class that feeds the hungry, volunteering with Habitat for Humanity, or donating your expertise in the name of a loved one.

By shifting the focus away from consumerism and toward contribution, you create a holiday experience that's deeply fulfilling—not just for you, but for those whose lives you touch.

Simplify Holiday Meals (Even If That Means Eating Out!)

For many people, holiday meals are the centerpiece of the celebration. But let's be real—preparing an elaborate holiday feast can be exhausting, especially if you're hosting and juggling other holiday obligations. If the idea of cooking a multicourse meal leaves you dreading the day, why not consider simplifying your holiday meals?

Eating out for a holiday meal—gasp!—might be just the solution to your holiday stress. While it may feel unconventional or even "wrong" to skip the home-cooked spread, eating out frees you from the burden of cooking and cleaning. It allows you to focus on the experience of sharing a meal together, rather than spending hours in the kitchen.

If dining out isn't your style, you can still simplify by opting for a potluck-style meal, where each guest brings a dish. Alternatively, you could choose to scale back on the number of dishes you prepare, focusing on just a few meaningful favorites rather than an overwhelming spread.

For those who feel the toll of the many "eating holidays" like Halloween, Thanksgiving, Christmas, Kwanzaa, and New Year's Eve, consider opting to celebrate with food on just one or two holidays rather than all of them. By doing this, you can take care of your health and well-being without feeling deprived. You can still enjoy festive meals—just in a way that feels balanced and sustainable for you.

Focus on Experiences and Connections

At the heart of every meaningful holiday season is connection. Whether it's with family, friends, or your community, the moments that matter most are often those shared with others—not the gifts exchanged or the elaborate decorations on display.

Consider ways you can shift the focus from materialism to shared experiences. This might mean gathering your loved ones for a cozy movie night, taking a family walk through a local park to enjoy the holiday lights, or spending a quiet evening reflecting on the past year together.

Instead of racing through tasks to achieve the perfect holiday, think about how you can slow down and create opportunities for meaningful conversation and connection. Ask your family members what they value most about the holidays and plan your activities around those answers. Maybe they don't care about the perfectly set table or the matching pajamas—instead, they might cherish the laughter that comes with a spontaneous game night or the warmth of an intimate dinner.

Set Boundaries Around Holiday Obligations

We often feel obligated to say yes to every holiday event, tradition, and social gathering. But by saying yes to everything, we can quickly overwhelm ourselves and lose sight of the meaningful moments we genuinely want to experience. Setting boundaries is essential to maintaining a sense of peace and balance during the holidays.

If your calendar is already full, give yourself permission to decline invitations that don't align with your priorities. Focus on the events and gatherings that bring you the most joy and let go of the rest. You can say no with grace by being honest and kind. Here's a simple script:

- "Thank you so much for inviting me! I've decided to keep things simple this year and focus on a few quiet evenings with family, but I hope you have a wonderful time."

By setting boundaries, you protect your time and energy, ensuring that the holidays remain a source of joy rather than stress. You also encourage others to do the same.

The Freedom of Letting Go: Let the Ducks Waddle

The holidays can feel overwhelming when we're trying to meet the programmed expectations placed on us by consumerism and societal norms. But when we let go of the need to follow a script—when we allow the ducks to waddle past without chasing them—we create space for a more authentic, fulfilling holiday experience.

It's okay if things aren't perfect. It's okay if you skip the holiday meal, simplify your gift-giving, or create new traditions that better align with your values. The most important thing is that you're creating a holiday season that feels *authentic* to you—one that prioritizes connection, joy, and meaning over perfection and obligation.

As you move forward, ask yourself, *"What truly matters to me this holiday season?"* Let your answer guide you and let go of the rest. The ducks can waddle, but you don't have to chase them. This holiday season, embrace the freedom that comes with living authentically, and savor the moments that bring you true joy.

Chapter 5

The Power of Pausing: Mindfulness Amid the Noise

*'Tis the gift to be simple, 'tis the gift to be free
'Tis the gift to come down where we ought to be.*
Simple Gifts (Brackett, 1848)

The holidays arrive at a time when the natural world slows down. In the Northern Hemisphere, days are shortest, nights are longest, and nature itself seems to retreat into a quiet, restful state. The trees are bare, the air is cooler, and animals—especially our pets—seem to instinctively know that this is a season for slowing down, resting, and rejuvenating.

Yet, for us humans, modern society sends a quite different message. Rather than heeding the call to rest, we're often caught in a whirlwind of activities and obligations. We try to pack more into each day—shopping, cooking, decorating, attending events—and the result is that by the time the holidays are over, many of us feel depleted and burned out. We've crammed so much into these shorter days that we barely have time to breathe.

But what if we approached the holiday season differently? What if, instead of racing against the clock, we honored the rhythms of nature and took our cues from the animals around us? What if we allowed ourselves to pause, to rest, and to savor the simple pleasures of the season? This is where *mindfulness* comes in. By practicing mindfulness, we can create more space for the things that truly matter, and we can reclaim the joy and peace that often get lost amid the holiday chaos.

In this chapter, we'll explore how mindfulness can help us navigate the holidays with greater ease, balance, and presence. We'll look at practical techniques for staying grounded and present, discuss how being mindful can enhance our experience of holiday moments, and offer simple mindfulness exercises that you can integrate into even the busiest of schedules. And as we'll see, sometimes the best way to honor the season is to simply slow down and do less.

Embracing the Rhythm of the Season

The holidays occur during a time when nature encourages us to *slow down*. The shorter days and longer nights are a signal that it's time to rest and reflect. Our own *circadian rhythms*, which are influenced by the natural light-dark cycle, also align with this slower pace. We're biologically wired to feel a bit more tired during this time of year, as the lack of sunlight prompts the production of melatonin, the hormone that regulates sleep.

Yet, instead of heeding this call for rest, modern society has us doing the opposite. We push ourselves to stay busy, cramming more into our schedules than ever before. We attend more parties, buy more gifts, and try to create a "perfect" holiday experience, all while the natural world is urging us to pause and reflect.

In contrast, our pets seem to understand this instinctively. If you have a cat curled up in a sunbeam or a dog lounging by the fire, you've probably noticed that they have no qualms about sleeping more and slowing down during the colder, darker months. They aren't worried about checking off holiday to-do lists; they're unapologetic about honoring their need for rest.

Taking a cue from nature and our pets, we can use the holiday season as an opportunity to embrace *stillness* and *contemplation*. Instead of fighting against the natural rhythm of the season, we can align ourselves with it, giving ourselves permission to rest, reflect, and take things a bit more slowly.

The Importance of Sunlight and Rest

While the shorter days and longer nights invite us to slow down, it's also important to get plenty of *sunlight* during the holiday season, especially if you live in a region where daylight is scarce. Exposure to natural light helps regulate our circadian rhythms and boosts our mood, making us feel good. Happiness then happens due to the increased production of the brain hormone serotonin. Even on colder days, spending time outdoors—whether it's a short walk in the morning or simply sitting by a window where the sunlight streams in—can make an enormous difference in how we feel.

Just as important as sunlight is *rest*. The holidays can be a demanding time, both physically and emotionally, so it's essential to listen to your body's signals and prioritize sleep. You don't have to do it all, and you certainly don't have to sacrifice rest in order to meet holiday expectations. As we'll explore later in this chapter, mindfulness can help you tune into your body's needs, allowing you to recognize when it's time to pause and recharge.

Mindfulness and Stress: Slowing Down Amid the Noise

The holidays can be a source of joy, but they can also bring a significant amount of stress and anxiety. The pressure to meet expectations, combined with the flurry of holiday activities, can leave us feeling overwhelmed and disconnected from the true meaning of the season. This is where mindfulness proves to be highly effective.

Mindfulness is the practice of staying fully engaged in the present moment. When we practice mindfulness, we slow down and connect with the present, rather than getting caught up in the worries of the future or the regrets of the past. This simple shift in focus can reduce stress, ease anxiety, and help us experience the holidays with more clarity and joy.

By incorporating mindfulness into your holiday routine, you can create moments of calm amid the noise. Whether it's through deep breathing, a mindful walk, or simply pausing to savor the experience of decorating the tree or sharing a meal, mindfulness allows you to slow down and reconnect with what truly matters.

The Science Behind Mindfulness and Stress Reduction

Mindfulness has been extensively researched for its ability to reduce stress and improve overall well-being (Kabat-Zinn, 2013). Studies have shown that mindfulness practices can

- **lower cortisol**, the hormone associated with stress (Hölzel et al., 2011).
- **improve emotional regulation**, helping you manage feelings of overwhelm or frustration (Guendelman, Medeiros, & Rampes, 2017).
- **enhance focus and attention**, allowing you to be more present with loved ones and fully enjoy the holiday moments (Jha, Krompinger, & Baime, 2007).
- **reduce symptoms of anxiety and depression**, contributing to a greater sense of peace and contentment (Hofmann, Sawyer, Witt, & Oh, 2010).

Incorporating even small moments of mindfulness into your day can have a profound impact on how you experience the holidays.

Practical Mindfulness Techniques for the Holidays

Staying mindful during the holiday season doesn't require hours of meditation or a complete lifestyle overhaul. In fact, mindfulness can be woven into your everyday routine, no matter how busy your schedule is. Here are some practical mindfulness techniques to help you stay grounded and present, even during the busiest of days.

Deep Breathing

When stress starts to build, one of the simplest and most effective mindfulness techniques is *deep breathing*. When we're anxious or overwhelmed, our breath tends to become shallow, which can increase feelings of tension. Taking a few slow, deep breaths can calm the nervous system and bring you back to the present moment.

How to Practice Counting Breaths:

1. Find a quiet spot or pause wherever you are.

2. Take a slow, deep breath in through your nose for a count of four, allowing your lungs to fully expand.

3. Pause and hold your breath for a count of four.

4. Slowly exhale through your mouth for a count of four, letting go of any tension.

5. Repeat this for five cycles, focusing on the sensation of the breath moving in and out of your body.

6. This exercise can be done anytime—whether you're waiting in line at a store, sitting in holiday traffic, or taking a brief pause between activities.

Mindful Walking

During the holidays, it's easy to feel like you're constantly rushing from one place to another. *Mindful walking* is a way to slow down and bring mindfulness into your daily movements, turning an ordinary walk into an opportunity to reconnect with the present moment.

How to Practice:

- As you walk, focus on being present, in the moment, each time your foot hits the ground.

- Pay attention to how your body moves with each step—how your legs and arms coordinate, how your weight shifts.
- Notice your surroundings: the sounds, the smells, the colors, the crispness of the air.
- If your mind starts to wander, gently bring your attention back to your steps and your breath.

You can practice mindful walking whether you're strolling through your neighborhood, walking to your car, or simply moving from one room to another. It's a simple but powerful way to bring presence into your day.

Savoring the Moment

The holidays are full of sensory experiences—the smell of fresh pine, the taste of a warm meal, the glow of candlelight. *Savoring the moment* is a mindfulness practice that helps you fully enjoy these experiences by paying close attention to them as they happen.

How to Practice:

When eating a holiday meal, pause before taking your first bite. Look at the food, notice the colors and textures. As you eat, focus on the flavors and how they change with each bite.

When you're with loved ones, focus on being fully present. Listen deeply to what they're saying, notice their expressions, and appreciate the connection.

As you decorate or admire holiday lights, take a moment to appreciate the beauty around you. Let yourself be fully absorbed in the colors, shapes, and warmth of the decorations.

By savoring these moments, you turn everyday activities into opportunities for mindfulness and gratitude.

Enhancing Holiday Moments With Mindfulness

Mindfulness doesn't just help you manage stress—it also enhances the quality of your holiday moments. When you're fully present, you're able to experience the holidays in a deeper, more meaningful way. Here's how mindfulness can transform ordinary holiday activities into moments of connection and joy:

- **Sharing a Meal:** Instead of rushing through the meal to get to the next activity, mindfulness helps you slow down and enjoy the flavors, the company, and the act of sharing food with loved ones. When you eat mindfully, you not only nourish your body but also your relationships.

- **Spending Time with Family:** Mindfulness helps you be fully present with the people you care about. Rather than being distracted by your phone or your to-do list, you can focus on meaningful conversations and deeper connections.

- **Admiring Decorations and Lights:** Rather than viewing decorating as just another task, mindfulness invites you to appreciate the beauty and symbolism of the holiday season. You might take a few moments to simply sit by the tree and enjoy the twinkling lights or breathe in the scent of holiday candles.

Simple Mindfulness Exercises for a Busy Schedule

Even in the middle of holiday preparations, there are small, simple ways to practice mindfulness. Here are a few exercises that you can integrate into your daily routine, no matter how hectic things get.

One-Minute Breathing

When you feel overwhelmed, take just one minute to focus on your breath. Close your eyes, allowing yourself to tune out the quacking duck distractions around you. Take a slow, deep breath in through your nose, feeling the air fill your lungs and expand your chest. Hold it for a moment, then gently release the breath, exhaling slowly and fully, letting any tension or stress flow out with it. As you exhale, feel your body relax and your mind begin to quiet. Repeat this for a minute, focusing only on your breathing. This quick reset can calm your mind and body.

Mindful Transitions

Use the moments between activities—whether you're walking from one room to another or waiting in line—to practice mindfulness. Focus on your breath or simply notice your surroundings. These small pauses can help you stay grounded throughout the day.

Gratitude Meditation

At the end of each day, take a few minutes to reflect on what you're grateful for. Sit quietly, close your eyes, and think about the people, experiences, or things that brought you joy that day. This practice helps cultivate positivity and appreciation, even during stressful times.

Mindful Eating

Before you begin a meal, pause and appreciate the food in front of you. Notice its colors, smells, and textures. As you eat, focus on each bite—savor the flavors, the sensations, and the nourishment it provides. This practice not only deepens your enjoyment of each meal but also keeps you grounded, helping you manage portion sizes and avoid mindless holiday snacking.

Conclusion: Pausing to Honor the Season

The holiday season is a time for joy, reflection, and connection—but only if we slow down enough to experience it. By practicing mindfulness, you can create more space for the moments that matter most. Whether it's through a simple deep breath, a mindful walk, or savoring a meal, these small pauses help you stay grounded amid the chaos and noise of the season.

Mindfulness is a gift you can give yourself during the holidays—a way to reconnect with your inner calm, honor the natural rhythm of the season, and create deeper, more meaningful moments with the people you love.

As you move forward, remember to take a moment each day to pause, breathe, and appreciate the present. After all, it's the quiet, mindful moments that truly make the holidays special.

Chapter 6

Breaking the Holiday Duck Cycle: How to Create Balance

*Peace on the earth, good will to men,
from heaven's all-gracious King.
The world in solemn stillness lay,
to hear the angels sing.*
It Came Upon a Midnight Clear (Sears, 1849)

The holiday season is supposed to be a time of joy, celebration, and connection. But more often than not, it can feel like a relentless cycle of obligations, to-do lists, and expectations. Balancing work, family, a social life, and self-care during the holidays can feel overwhelming, as though you're constantly juggling too many "ducks"—those little tasks and commitments that seem to multiply at this time of year. And when we try to do it all, we often end up sacrificing our energy, our peace of mind, and our enjoyment of the season.

In this chapter, we'll explore the idea of *balance* during the holidays, but not in the way you might think.

Achieving balance is not about doing everything equally or managing time perfectly. Instead, it's about managing your *energy*—knowing where to invest it and where to conserve it. It's about recognizing that it's okay to let some of those holiday ducks go and focusing on the things that truly bring you joy, meaning, and connection.

We'll cover practical strategies for letting go of unnecessary tasks, managing energy more effectively, and delegating responsibilities, so you can navigate the holiday season with more ease and less stress. With these tools, you'll be able to break the holiday duck cycle and create a sense of balance that supports your well-being and enhances your enjoyment of the holidays.

Rethinking Balance: It's About Energy, Not Time

One of the most common misconceptions about balance is that it's about perfectly dividing your time between all the areas of your life. But the reality is, time is a finite resource—you only have so many hours in a day, especially during the holidays when extra tasks and events are added to your schedule. If you focus solely on managing your time, you'll likely feel frustrated, because there's simply not enough time to do it all.

The key to true balance isn't about how much time you have, but how you manage your *energy*. Energy, unlike time, is a renewable resource. By conserving your energy and being intentional about where you invest it, you can create a sense of balance that leaves you feeling more refreshed, focused, and present. When you think in terms of energy rather than time, you begin to realize that balance is about making choices that align with your priorities and your well-being.

The Energy Equation: Where to Invest and Where to Conserve

The holiday season is full of opportunities to invest your energy—into family, social events, work, and self-care. But not all tasks are created equal. Some activities energize you, while others drain you. The trick is learning how to *prioritize* the things that replenish your energy and let go of the tasks that deplete it.

Here's how to start:

1. **Identify Your Energy Drains and Boosters**
Take a moment to reflect on the activities and obligations that fill your holiday season. Which ones leave you feeling drained and exhausted? Which ones make you feel uplifted, connected, and energized? For example, hosting a large holiday dinner might be something you enjoy, but if it's causing you stress, it's an energy drain. On the other hand, spending time with a close friend over coffee might be an energy booster.

2. **Conserve Energy by Letting Go of Unnecessary Tasks**
Once you've identified your energy drains, consider how you can either *delegate*, *simplify*, or *eliminate* them altogether. Letting go of tasks that don't serve your well-being or align with your priorities frees up energy for the things that truly matter.

3. **Invest Energy in What Matters Most**
Prioritize the activities, traditions, and experiences that bring you joy, fulfillment, and a sense of connection. These are the areas

where your energy is well-spent. Whether it's quality time with family, practicing self-care, or attending a holiday event that you genuinely enjoy, invest your energy wisely.

Strategies for Balancing Obligations and Joy

During the holidays, it can feel like you're constantly torn between your obligations (family gatherings, work deadlines, gift shopping) and your desire for joy (rest, meaningful connection, personal enjoyment). Finding balance between these competing demands is key to creating a holiday season that feels fulfilling rather than exhausting.

Learn to Let Some Ducks Go

One of the most important lessons of balance is that *you don't have to do it all*. The pressure to attend every event, buy every gift, or participate in every tradition can weigh heavily during the holidays. But balance comes from recognizing that it's okay to let some things go. You don't need to chase every duck—especially the ones that don't bring you joy or add value to your holiday experience.

- **Holiday Events:** If your calendar is packed with parties, gatherings, and obligations, ask yourself, "Which events are truly meaningful to me?" Which ones feel like obligations? Give yourself permission to say no to the events that don't align with your priorities, even if it feels uncomfortable at first.

- **Traditions:** Just because something is a tradition doesn't mean it has to be done every year, especially if it no longer brings you joy. Take stock of your holiday traditions and decide which ones are worth keeping and which ones you can let go. Perhaps this year, you can simplify by focusing on one or two meaningful traditions rather than trying to uphold them all.

Set Boundaries with Family and Work

The holidays often come with heightened expectations, particularly when it comes to family and work obligations. It's easy to feel like you have to be everything to everyone, but setting clear boundaries is essential for maintaining balance.

- **Family Boundaries:** If you find yourself stretched thin by family commitments, it's okay to set boundaries around how much time and energy you can give. For example, if hosting the entire family for days on end is overwhelming, consider hosting a shorter gathering or asking guests to help with meals and cleanup.

- **Work Boundaries:** The end of the year often brings work deadlines and additional pressure, but it's important to create boundaries around your work time, especially if you're trying to balance it with holiday obligations. Set clear expectations with your employer or colleagues about when you'll be available and when you'll be offline to focus on family or self-care.

Practice the "Joy-to-Obligation" Ratio

To create a more balanced holiday season, try practicing the "joy-to-obligation" ratio. For every obligation you take on—whether it's attending a work party, baking cookies for your child's school, or running last-minute errands—balance it with something that brings you joy.

This helps ensure that your holiday experience isn't all about meeting other people's expectations but includes moments that fill your own cup.

- **For example:** If you're attending a holiday event that feels more like a duty than a delight, balance it by setting aside time for an activity you enjoy—whether it's watching a favorite holiday movie, reading a book, or going for a walk in the fresh air. By consciously including joy in your holiday routine, you're less likely to feel weighed down by obligations.

Practical Tips for Time Management and Energy Preservation

Finding balance during the holidays isn't just about managing your obligations—it's also about using your time and energy wisely. Here are some practical tips for conserving energy and managing your holiday schedule without feeling overwhelmed.

Use the Power of Delegation

One of the simplest ways to conserve energy during the holidays is to delegate tasks. You don't have to be responsible for everything. Whether it's asking family members to help with decorating, dividing up the cooking for holiday meals, or enlisting help with gift wrapping, delegation allows you to share the workload.

- **How to Delegate:** Be specific when asking for help. Instead of saying, "I could use some help with the holiday party," say, "Can you handle the appetizers while I prepare the main course?" People are often more willing to help when they know exactly what's needed.

Simplify Your To-Do List

It's easy to feel like everything on your holiday to-do list is a must-do. But in reality, many of the things we think we *have* to do are optional. Take a look at your to-do list and ask yourself, "What can be simplified, postponed, or eliminated altogether?"

- **For example:** Instead of baking five distinct types of cookies, choose one favorite recipe and stick with that. Instead of buying elaborate, time-consuming gifts, consider giving simpler, more meaningful presents, like a heartfelt letter or a donation to a charity in the recipient's name.

Prioritize Self-Care

During the holiday season, it's easy to neglect your own well-being in favor of taking care of others. But self-care is essential for maintaining balance and managing stress. Make self-care a priority by scheduling time for rest, relaxation, and activities that recharge your energy.

- **Self-Care Ideas:** This could be as simple as taking a warm bath at the end of a busy day, going for a walk in the sunlight, or practicing mindfulness to help you stay present. Remember, self-care isn't selfish—it's necessary for keeping yourself healthy and balanced.

Create Buffer Time

One of the easiest ways to conserve energy is to build *buffer time* into your holiday schedule. Instead of packing your days back-to-back with activities and errands, allow for gaps between tasks where you can rest, regroup, and recharge. This prevents you from feeling rushed and gives you time to breathe between obligations.

- **For example:** If you know you have a busy day of holiday shopping or family gatherings, schedule 15-20 minutes of downtime afterward to sit quietly, enjoy a cup of tea, or simply relax. These small pauses can make an enormous difference in how you feel at the end of the day.

Focus on Progress, Not Perfection

During the holidays, it's easy to fall into the trap of perfectionism—trying to make every meal flawless, every gift perfectly wrapped, and every event perfectly planned. But striving for perfection only leads to stress and burnout. Instead, focus on *progress*—getting things done in a way that's "good enough" without overextending yourself.

- **For example:** If the decorations aren't exactly how you envisioned, that's okay. If the meal doesn't turn out perfectly, that's okay too. What matters is that you're present and enjoying the moment, not that everything looks or feels perfect.

Conclusion: Finding Your Holiday Balance

Achieving balance during the holidays doesn't mean doing everything perfectly or managing your time with precision. It's about being intentional with your *energy*—knowing when to conserve it, where to invest it, and how to let go of the tasks that drain you. By letting some ducks waddle by and focusing on what truly matters, you can create a holiday season that feels joyful, meaningful, and manageable.

Remember, balance is not about doing everything. It's about doing what matters most and giving yourself the grace to let go of the rest. By prioritizing your well-being, setting boundaries, and practicing self-care, you'll find that you have more energy to fully enjoy the holidays—without feeling overwhelmed by obligations.

As you move forward, consider what balance looks like for you this holiday season. What can you let go of? Where can you conserve your energy? And how can you create moments of joy, rest, and connection amid the holiday noise? With these questions in mind, you'll be well on your way to breaking the holiday duck cycle and creating a more peaceful, balanced season.

Chapter 7

Don't Feed the Ducks: Protecting Your Mental Health

*Then let us all rejoice again
On Christmas Day, on Christmas Day
Then let us all rejoice again
On Christmas Day in the morning.*
(Traditional, n.d.)

The holidays are often portrayed as the most wonderful time of the year, filled with joy, laughter, and celebration. But for many people, the reality is more complicated. The demands of the holiday season—combined with heightened expectations, social obligations, and financial pressures—can take a serious toll on your mental health. What's supposed to be a season of connection and joy can quickly turn into one of stress, anxiety, and overwhelm.

The accumulation of small stressors—those "ducks" we've been talking about—can peck away at your peace of mind, leaving you feeling depleted before the season even gets into full swing. From managing family dynamics to balancing work responsibilities with holiday preparations, the sheer volume of tasks and expectations can cause even the most festive person to feel burned out.

In this chapter, we'll explore how holiday stress impacts your mental health and offer strategies for protecting yourself from feeling overwhelmed. You'll learn how to recognize the early signs of stress and burnout, and we'll share practical techniques for emotional regulation, including journaling, talking to a therapist, and setting aside quiet time for reflection. We'll also discuss how to cultivate a supportive environment with family and friends, and how to ask for help when you need it.

By learning to recognize and manage holiday stress, you can reclaim your mental well-being and experience a holiday season that nurtures rather than drains you.

How Holiday Stress Impacts Mental Health

The holidays are a time of increased social interactions, financial pressure, and, for many, a relentless to-do list. Even if you love the holiday season, these factors can add significant stress to your life, impacting your mental health. One of the biggest challenges is that stress during the holidays often accumulates gradually. It starts small—an extra errand here, a last-minute invitation there—but over time, these little stressors build up, leaving you feeling overwhelmed, exhausted, or even anxious and depressed.

Accumulating Stressors: The Pecking of Holiday Ducks

Just like a flock of ducks nibbling away at your peace, the small, persistent stressors of the holidays can gradually wear you down. These stressors might seem trivial on their own, but when combined, they create a cumulative effect that can feel overwhelming. Common holiday stressors include:

- **Financial Pressures:** The pressure to buy gifts, attend events, and host parties can create significant financial strain, leading to anxiety about money and debt.

- **Family Dynamics:** Spending extended time with family can lead to reminders of old conflicts or unresolved issues, making gatherings more stressful than enjoyable.

- **Time Management:** Balancing work, family, and social commitments during the holidays can leave you feeling like there's never enough time to get everything done.

- **Social Obligations:** From office parties to neighborhood events, the pressure to attend every gathering can be exhausting, especially for those who are more introverted or who feel socially anxious.

- **Perfectionism:** The expectation to create a "perfect" holiday experience—for yourself, your family, or your friends—can lead to feelings of inadequacy, especially when things don't go as planned.

When these stressors pile up, it's easy to feel like you're being pecked at from all sides. If left unchecked, this cumulative stress can lead to mental health issues such as anxiety, depression, or burnout.

Recognizing the Signs of Overwhelm and Burnout

The first step in protecting your mental health during the holidays is recognizing the signs of overwhelm and burnout early on. When we're caught up in the busyness of the season, it can be easy to ignore or dismiss the warning signs that our mental health is suffering. However, the sooner you recognize these signs, the sooner you can take steps to manage your stress and prevent it from escalating.

Common Signs of Overwhelm

- **Irritability or Mood Swings:** You might find yourself feeling unusually anxious, short-tempered, or snapping at others more often than usual.

- **Physical Symptoms:** Stress often manifests in the body, leading to headaches, stomachaches, muscle tension, or fatigue.

- **Difficulty Concentrating:** You may find it harder to focus on tasks or feel like your mind is constantly racing with to-do lists and worries.

- **Sleep Disturbances:** Trouble falling asleep, staying asleep, or waking up feeling unrefreshed are common signs of stress.

- **Withdrawal From Social Activities:** If you start avoiding social events or isolating yourself, it may be a sign that the holiday stress is becoming too much.

- **Feeling Emotionally Drained:** A sense of emotional exhaustion or a lack of enthusiasm for activities you usually enjoy can signal burnout.

If you recognize any of these signs in yourself, it's important to take them seriously. Ignoring the early signs of stress and burnout can lead to more serious mental health issues, so it's essential to address them as soon as they arise.

Techniques for Protecting Your Mental Health

Once you've recognized that holiday stress is affecting your mental health, the next step is to take proactive steps to protect yourself. The good news is that there are many simple and effective techniques you can use to manage stress, regulate your emotions, and maintain your mental well-being throughout the holiday season.

Journaling for Emotional Clarity

One of the most powerful tools for emotional regulation is *journaling*. Writing down your thoughts and feelings allows you to process your emotions and gain clarity about what's truly bothering you. Journaling also helps to release pent-up stress and tension, giving you a healthy outlet for your emotions.

How to Practice Journaling:

1. Set aside 10-15 minutes each day to write in a journal, either in the morning or before bed.

2. Write freely about what's on your mind—don't worry about grammar or structure. The goal is to express your emotions, not to create a polished piece of writing.

3. If you're not sure where to start, try answering prompts like, "What is causing me the most stress right now? How can I let go of this stress? What am I grateful for today?"

Journaling regularly during the holidays can help you stay connected to your emotions, prevent overwhelm, and give you a clearer sense of how to move forward.

Talk to a Therapist or Trusted Friend

The holidays can bring up a range of emotions—some joyful, others more complicated. If you find that holiday stress is becoming overwhelming, consider talking to a therapist or confiding in a trusted friend. Sometimes, just expressing your thoughts aloud can be incredibly relieving.

- **Therapy:** A licensed therapist can provide guidance on managing stress, navigating family dynamics, and improving emotional regulation. They can also help you develop coping strategies that work specifically for you.

- **Trusted Friends or Family:** If therapy isn't an option, talking to a trusted friend or family member can be equally beneficial. Choose someone who will listen without judgment and offer support without trying to "fix" your situation.

Seeking support is a true display of strength, not a sign of weakness. Opening up about your challenges, whether to a professional or a caring friend, can ease the emotional burden and remind you that you're not alone.

Set Aside Quiet Time for Reflection

In the midst of holiday busyness, it's easy to get caught up in doing and forget about being. Setting aside *quiet time for reflection* is a valuable way to reset your mind and reconnect with yourself. Whether it's through meditation, prayer, or simply sitting quietly with your thoughts, this time allows you to process your emotions and release stress.

Ideas for Quiet Reflection

- **Mindfulness Meditation:** Set aside 5-10 minutes each day to sit quietly and focus on your breath. If you notice your mind drifting, calmly guide your attention back to the present moment. This practice can help you stay grounded and reduce feelings of anxiety.

- **Gratitude Practice:** Set aside a few minutes each day to pause and reflect on the things you're grateful for. Whether it's the small joys or the bigger blessings in your life, taking this time to focus on gratitude can shift your perspective, uplift your mood, and cultivate a deeper sense of contentment. By regularly acknowledging these positive aspects, you're also training your mind to notice and appreciate the goodness around you, even in challenging times. Focusing on the positive aspects of your life can help shift your mindset and reduce stress.

- **Nature Walks:** Spending time in nature is a powerful way to quiet the mind and reconnect with yourself. Even a short walk outside can help you feel more grounded and centered.

These moments of stillness can be especially helpful during the holiday season when things tend to move at a fast pace. They provide a necessary break from the noise and allow you to check in with how you're feeling.

Cultivating a Supportive Environment

Your environment plays a significant role in your mental well-being, and during the holidays, it's important to surround yourself with people who support you. Cultivating a supportive environment—both at home and in your social circles—can help you manage stress more effectively and create a sense of emotional safety.

Communicate Your Needs to Family and Friends

One of the biggest sources of holiday stress can be feeling like you have to meet everyone else's expectations. To protect your mental health, it's important to communicate your needs clearly and honestly with the people around you. Let your family and friends know if you're feeling overwhelmed, and don't be afraid to ask for what you need—whether it's help with holiday preparations, more alone time, or simply a break from socializing.

- **Example:** "I've been feeling really stressed with everything going on, and I'd love some help with preparing dinner this year. Could you bring a side dish or dessert?"
- **Example:** "I'm feeling a little overwhelmed with all the social events. I think I'll skip the party this weekend and take some time to recharge."

When you communicate your needs openly, you give others the opportunity to support you, and you set the stage for healthier, more balanced interactions.

Ask for Help When You Need It

Asking for help can be challenging, especially if you're used to doing everything on your own. But during the holidays, trying to do it all without support can lead to burnout. Whether it's help with holiday tasks, emotional support, or simply a listening ear, don't hesitate to reach out when you need it.

- **Delegate Tasks:** If you're hosting a holiday gathering, ask family members to help with cooking, decorating, or cleaning up. If you're overwhelmed with gift shopping, consider asking a partner or friend to help you pick out presents or wrap gifts.

- **Emotional Support:** If you're feeling emotionally drained, reach out to a close friend or family member for support. Simply talking about your feelings can help relieve some of the stress you're carrying.

Keep in mind that you don't have to navigate the holiday season by yourself. Asking for help is a sign of self-awareness and strength, and it allows you to conserve your energy for the things that matter most.

Create Boundaries Around Stressful Situations

If certain family dynamics, social events, or holiday obligations are particularly stressful for you, it's important to set boundaries. Boundaries help protect your mental health by creating clear limits around what you're willing to take on—and what you're not.

- **Example:** If spending extended periods of time with extended family is stressful, consider setting a time limit for how long you'll stay at family gatherings. You can express this boundary gently: "I'll be there for dinner, but I'm going to leave afterward to get some rest."

- **Example:** If gift shopping is overwhelming, set a clear budget and stick to it. Let your family know that you're simplifying this year: "We're doing smaller, meaningful gifts this year so we can focus more on spending time together."

Boundaries are not about shutting people out—they're about protecting your well-being and creating a holiday experience that feels healthy and manageable for you.

Conclusion: Nurturing Your Mental Health During the Holidays

The holidays can be a wonderful time of joy and connection, but they can also bring significant stress and overwhelm. Protecting your mental health during this season is essential for ensuring that you can enjoy the holidays in a way that feels meaningful and fulfilling.

By recognizing the signs of stress and burnout early on, practicing techniques for emotional regulation, and cultivating a supportive environment, you can navigate the holidays with more ease and balance. Remember, it's okay to say no, ask for help, and take time for yourself. Your mental health is just as important as any holiday tradition or obligation—and by prioritizing it, you'll find that you're able to experience the season with more peace, clarity, and joy.

As you move forward, make a commitment to "not feed the ducks"—to not let small stressors accumulate to the point of overwhelm. Instead, focus on what truly matters to you, protect your energy, and give yourself the grace to rest when you need it.

Chapter 8

Tending to Your Own Nest: Self-Care During the Holidays

Silent night, holy night!
All is calm, all is bright.
(Mohr & Gruber, 1818)

The holiday season is a time of giving—to family, to friends, to work obligations, and to holiday traditions. But amid all this giving, it's easy to forget one of the most important gifts: the gift of caring for yourself. With so many responsibilities pulling you in different directions, self-care can easily fall by the wayside, treated as a luxury rather than a necessity. Yet, the truth is that *self-care is essential*—especially during the busy holiday season.

When you neglect self-care, you're more likely to feel overwhelmed, stressed, and run-down. And while it might seem like there's no time for self-care during such a hectic period, the reality is that taking care of yourself is what enables you to manage holiday demands more effectively. *Self-care isn't selfish*—it's how you refill your energy, regain balance, and maintain your mental, emotional, and physical well-being. When you're at your best, you're better equipped to handle everything the holidays throw at you, from family gatherings to last-minute shopping trips.

In this chapter, we'll explore the importance of self-care during the holidays and offer a variety of self-care practices you can integrate into your routine—whether you have five minutes or a few hours to spare. You'll learn how to prioritize self-care without feeling guilty or neglecting your responsibilities, and how to see it as an essential part of thriving, not just surviving, during the holiday season.

The Importance of Self-Care During the Holidays

The holidays are a time of heightened demands—more social events, more tasks to complete, more people to please. It's easy to get caught up in the holiday hustle and neglect yourself. Yet, when you don't prioritize self-care, the holiday season can quickly become exhausting, leaving you feeling burned out before it's even over.

Why Self-Care Matters During the Holidays:

- **Stress Management:** The holidays bring extra stress, from planning family gatherings to managing gift shopping. Without self-care, stress can escalate, affecting both your mental and physical health.

- **Emotional Resilience:** Holidays can trigger complicated emotions—family tensions, financial worries, or even loneliness. Practicing self-care helps you build emotional resilience, making it easier to navigate these challenges.

- **Physical Well-Being:** The holiday season often involves a change in routine—late nights, indulgent meals, and less time for exercise or rest. Taking care of your body through proper nutrition, movement, and sleep is essential for staying healthy.

- **Replenishing Energy:** Giving to others is a beautiful part of the holiday spirit, but you can't give from an empty cup. Self-care refills your energy, allowing you to be fully present with the people and activities that matter most.

When you make self-care a priority, you create a solid foundation for navigating the holiday season with greater ease and joy. You're better able to show up for your loved ones, handle stress, and enjoy the moments that make the holidays special.

Self-Care Is Essential, Not Indulgent

One of the biggest misconceptions about self-care is that it's a luxury—something indulgent that you only do when you have extra time or when everything else on your to-do list is done. But this mindset can lead to burnout, especially during the holidays. In reality, self-care is a *necessity*, not a luxury.

Self-care doesn't need to be complicated or take up a lot of time. It can be as simple as taking a few moments each day to check in with yourself, breathe deeply, or enjoy a quiet cup of tea. The key is to see self-care as an essential part of your daily routine—something that helps you stay grounded, balanced, and energized.

By shifting your mindset to view self-care as a necessity, you're more likely to prioritize it, even when your schedule is packed. And when you take care of yourself, you'll find that you have more energy and patience for the people and activities around you.

Simple Daily Self-Care Rituals

Even on the busiest days, you can practice small acts of self-care that help you reset and recharge. Here are a few simple self-care rituals that take only a few minutes but can make a significant difference in how you feel.

Morning Mindfulness

Start your day with a few moments of mindfulness to center yourself before the holiday chaos begins. Whether it's through deep breathing, meditation, or simply sitting quietly with a cup of coffee, this practice helps you approach the day with calm and focus.

How to Practice:

- Set aside five minutes each morning to sit quietly and breathe deeply.

- While you breathe, concentrate on the feeling of air flowing in and out of your body.

- If your thoughts begin to drift, gently guide your attention back to your breath.

- This practice sets a calm tone for the rest of your day, helping you navigate holiday stress with more ease.

Mindful Breaks

Throughout the day, take short breaks to check in with yourself and release any tension that's building up. Even a two-minute pause can help you reset and recharge.

How to Practice:

- Pause for a mindful break between tasks or errands.
- Close your eyes, take a deep breath, and ask yourself, "How am I feeling right now? What do I need in this moment?"
- If you feel tension in your body, gently stretch or move to release it.
- These brief moments of mindfulness help you stay present and connected to your needs throughout the day.

Gratitude Journaling

Every evening, pause a few moments to reflect on the things you're thankful for. Practicing gratitude is a powerful way to shift your focus from stress to appreciation, even during the busiest times.

How to Practice:

- Keep a small notebook by your bed, and each night, write down three things you're grateful for that day.
- They don't have to be big or significant—small moments of joy or connection are just as valuable.

- This simple practice helps you cultivate a sense of contentment and positivity, no matter how stressful your day has been.

Nourishing Your Body

During the holidays, it's easy to neglect your physical well-being in the rush to get things done. But taking care of your body is one of the most important forms of self-care. Simple practices like staying hydrated, eating nourishing foods, and getting enough sleep can make a substantial difference in how you feel.

How to Practice:

- Drink plenty of water throughout the day to stay hydrated.//
- Choose nourishing meals that fuel your body and give you sustained energy.
- Set a bedtime routine that helps you wind down and get quality sleep.
- Even small adjustments, like drinking an extra glass of water or going to bed 30 minutes earlier, can have a positive impact on your energy and mood.

Restorative Self-Care Practices

While daily self-care rituals help you maintain balance, it's also important to incorporate more *restorative practices* that allow you to fully recharge. These activities might require more time, but they're essential for deep rest and renewal, especially during the holidays.

Spa or Self-Care Days

Set aside time for a self-care day or half-day where you focus entirely on relaxation and rejuvenation. Whether it's a visit to a spa, a long bath at home, or simply spending the day in comfortable clothes, dedicating time to yourself is a powerful way to restore your energy.

Ideas for a Self-Care Day:

- Treat yourself to a massage, facial, or spa treatment.
- Create a spa experience at home with candles, soothing music, and a warm bath.
- Spend the day doing activities that relax and nourish you, whether it's reading, listening to music, or taking a leisurely walk.

Digital Detox

One of the biggest sources of stress during the holidays is the constant bombardment of notifications, emails, and social media updates. Taking a break from screens—whether for a few hours or a full day—can help you reset your mind and reduce anxiety.

How to Practice:

- Set specific times during the day when you'll step away from your phone, email, and social media.
- Use that time to engage in offline activities that relax and refresh you, such as reading, journaling, or spending time outdoors.

- Consider having a "digital detox" day where you disconnect entirely and focus on being present with yourself and your loved ones.

Exercise and Movement

Physical activity is a powerful form of self-care that not only benefits your body but also your mind. During the holidays, it's easy to let exercise fall by the wayside, but even small amounts of movement can boost your mood, increase your energy, and reduce stress.

How to Practice:

- Find an activity that you enjoy, whether it's walking, yoga, dancing, or a workout class.

- Aim for at least 20-30 minutes of movement each day, but don't stress if you can't do a full workout—short bursts of activity, like a 10-minute walk, still count.

- Exercise not only helps you stay physically healthy, but it also releases endorphins, which improve your mood and reduce feelings of stress and anxiety.

Connection and Play

Self-care isn't just about rest and relaxation—it's also about connection and play. Spending time with people who uplift and support you, or engaging in activities that bring you joy, is an essential part of nurturing your mental and emotional well-being.

How to Practice:

- Schedule time to connect with friends or family members who make you feel good. Whether it's

- a phone call, a coffee date, or a shared meal, these moments of connection help strengthen relationships and provide emotional support.
- Incorporate play into your routine—do something just for fun, whether it's playing a board game, going to a holiday event, or engaging in a creative activity like painting or crafting.

Laughter and joy are powerful forms of self-care that can shift your mindset and bring lightness to even the most stressful days.

Integrating Self-Care into Your Holiday Routine

One of the biggest challenges of self-care during the holidays is finding time for it without feeling guilty or neglecting your responsibilities. The key is to *integrate self-care into your existing routine* rather than treating it as something extra. By making small adjustments and building self-care into your daily life, you can nurture yourself without sacrificing your holiday obligations.

Plan for Self-Care

Just like you schedule holiday activities and events, schedule self-care into your calendar. Treat it as a non-negotiable part of your day, even if it's just 10-15 minutes. By planning for self-care, you're more likely to follow through on it, and you'll have a reminder to take time for yourself amid the holiday busyness.

- **Example:** Block out time in your calendar for a morning meditation, an evening bath, or a weekend walk.

Involve Your Family in Self-Care

Self-care doesn't have to be a solo activity. Involving your family or friends in self-care practices can make it easier to fit them into your routine and create shared moments of relaxation and connection.

- **Example:** Take a family walk after dinner or set aside time for a "quiet hour" where everyone engages in a relaxing activity, like reading or drawing.

Let Go of Guilt

One of the biggest barriers to self-care during the holidays is guilt. You might feel like taking time for yourself is selfish or that it's taking away from your responsibilities. But self-care is what allows you to show up fully for the people and activities you care about. When you prioritize your well-being, you're better able to handle the demands of the season with patience, energy, and joy.

- **Affirmation:** Whenever guilt arises, remind yourself: *Taking care of myself allows me to take care of others. My well-being matters.*

Practice "Good Enough" Self-Care

Self-care doesn't have to be perfect. If you can't fit in a full workout, a short walk is still valuable. If you don't have time for a long meditation, a few deep breaths can still make a difference. Let go of the idea that self-care needs to be elaborate or time-consuming. Even small, imperfect acts of self-care are meaningful and beneficial.

Conclusion: Self-Care as a Foundation for Thriving

The holidays are a time of giving, but the most important gift you can give yourself is the gift of self-care. By tending to your own nest—taking time to rest, recharge, and nourish your body and mind—you create the foundation for thriving during the holiday season.

Self-care isn't about escaping your responsibilities or being selfish—it's about making sure you're able to meet the demands of the holidays with energy, balance, and joy. By integrating small, meaningful self-care practices into your routine, you'll find that you're better equipped to handle the challenges of the season and fully enjoy the moments that matter most.

As you move forward, remember that self-care is not an indulgence—it's essential. Give yourself permission to prioritize your well-being, and trust that when you take care of yourself, everything else will fall into place. This holiday season, tend to your own nest, and let self-care be the gift that sustains you.

Chapter 9

Letting the Ducks Go: Moving Beyond the Holidays

*Christmas is coming, the goose is getting fat.
Please put a penny in the old man's hat
If you haven't got a penny, [then] a ha'penny will do.
If you haven't got a ha'penny, [then] God bless you!*
(Traditional, 1885)

The holidays are often described as a whirlwind—a chaotic blend of celebration, obligation, joy, and stress. By the time they end, many of us feel like we've been swept along in the current, barely able to catch our breath. But as the decorations come down and life returns to its regular rhythm, we're left with a valuable opportunity for reflection.

This chapter is about taking a step back after the holidays, letting go of what no longer serves you, and carrying forward the lessons you've learned. The mindset of letting go of small stressors—the ducks that crowd your life—doesn't have to be limited to the holiday season. It's a practice you can adopt year-round to cultivate peace, balance, and joy in your life.

In this last chapter, we'll explore how to reflect on the holiday season, identifying what worked well and what didn't. We'll also discuss how to apply the lessons you've learned to create a more balanced and fulfilling life beyond the holidays. You'll find exercises for setting realistic goals and intentions for the new year, with a focus on avoiding burnout and maintaining balance. Let's look at how to let go of those ducks and embrace a new year of clarity, intention, and self-care.

Post-Holiday Reflection: Learning From the Season

As the holiday season ends, it's tempting to dive straight into the new year without looking back. But taking time to reflect on your holiday experience can provide valuable insights that will help you navigate future holiday seasons—and life in general—with greater ease and balance.

Reflection Exercise: What Worked, What Didn't?

Before moving on from the holidays, take a moment to reflect on how things went. Set aside some quiet time with a journal or notebook and ask yourself the following questions. Be honest with your answers—this reflection is an opportunity for growth, not judgment.

- **What brought me joy during the holidays?** Reflect on the moments that made you feel genuinely happy, connected, or at peace. These might be simple moments, like a quiet morning walk or sharing a meal with loved ones, or bigger events, like a successful family gathering.

- **What caused me the most stress?**
  Think about the tasks, obligations, or expectations that drained your energy or caused unnecessary stress. Was it trying to create the perfect holiday meal? Attending too many social events? Managing difficult family dynamics?

- **What did I let go of, and how did it feel?**
  Consider the things you intentionally let go of this holiday season—whether it was saying no to an event, simplifying gift-giving, or delegating tasks. How did it feel to release those stressors? Did it make the holidays more enjoyable?

- **What could I do differently next time?**
  Reflect on what you'd like to improve or change for future holiday seasons. This might include setting clearer boundaries, simplifying your schedule, or prioritizing self-care.

- **How did self-care play a role in my holiday experience?**
  Think about how well you prioritized self-care during the holidays. Did you make time for rest and rejuvenation, or did it fall by the wayside? How can you integrate more self-care into future holiday seasons?

Integrating Lessons From the Holidays Into Your Life

The insights you gain from this reflection can help you make meaningful changes, not only during future holidays but throughout the year. The mindset of letting go, simplifying, and prioritizing your well-being is one that can serve you long after the holiday lights have dimmed.

Letting Go Year-Round: Carrying the Holiday Mindset Forward

The practice of letting go—of unnecessary stress, perfectionism, and obligations—doesn't have to be limited to the holidays. In fact, the lessons you've learned during the holiday season can be applied to your everyday life. By carrying this mindset forward, you can create a more balanced, peaceful, and fulfilling life throughout the year.

Let Go of Perfectionism

One of the biggest stressors during the holidays is the pressure to make everything perfect—whether it's the decorations, the meals, or the gifts. But as you likely discovered, perfectionism often leads to burnout rather than joy. Carrying the mindset of "good enough" into the new year can help you let go of unrealistic expectations and create more space for peace and enjoyment.

- **Practice:** The next time you find yourself striving for perfection, pause and ask yourself, "Is this effort really necessary? Will anyone notice if it's not perfect?" Then, consciously choose to do the best you can without overextending yourself.

Simplify Your To-Do List

During the holidays, you may have learned the value of simplifying your tasks—whether that meant delegating, saying no, or cutting back on unnecessary obligations. This practice of simplification can be a game-changer in your everyday life as well. By focusing on what truly matters and letting go of the rest, you'll free up time and energy for the things that bring you joy.

- **Practice:** Each week, review your to-do list and ask yourself, "What can I let go of? What's truly important?" Simplify your schedule by eliminating or delegating tasks that aren't essential.

Prioritize Self-Care and Rest

Self-care is often neglected during the holidays, but it's just as important—if not more so—during the rest of the year. Make a commitment to prioritize self-care as part of your regular routine, whether it's through daily rituals like mindfulness or more restorative practices like taking time off or spending a day focused on relaxation.

- **Practice:** Schedule self-care into your calendar just like any other appointment. Whether it's a daily meditation, a weekly walk, or a monthly spa day, treat self-care as non-negotiable.

Cultivate Boundaries

If you learned to set boundaries during the holidays—whether with family, work, or social obligations—don't stop there. Carry those boundaries into your everyday life. Boundaries are essential for protecting your energy and mental health year-round.

- **Practice:** Reflect on the boundaries you set during the holidays and consider how they can be applied to other areas of your life. For example, if you set limits on social events during the holidays, you might continue to limit how many social obligations you take on each month.

Setting Realistic Goals for the New Year

As you move beyond the holiday season and into the new year, it's tempting to set ambitious resolutions or goals. But all too often, these resolutions are rooted in perfectionism or unrealistic expectations, leading to burnout and disappointment. Instead of setting lofty goals that feel overwhelming, focus on creating *realistic, meaningful goals* that align with your values and support your well-being.

Reflect on Your Priorities

Before setting goals for the new year, take some time to reflect on what's profoundly important to you. What are your core values? What brings you joy and fulfillment? Use these reflections to guide your goal-setting process.

- **Exercise:** Write down your top three priorities for the new year. These could be related to your health, relationships, career, or personal growth. Once you've identified your priorities, set goals that align with them.

Set SMART Goals

To avoid burnout, it's important to set goals that are *specific, measurable, achievable, relevant, and time-bound* (SMART). This framework helps you create goals that are realistic and actionable, rather than overwhelming or vague.

- **Example:** Instead of setting a goal like "Get healthier," use the SMART framework to set a specific goal: "Walk for 30 minutes three times a week." This goal is specific, measurable, achievable, relevant to your health, and time-bound.

Focus on Progress, Not Perfection

The mindset of letting go of perfectionism applies to goal-setting as well. Rather than striving for perfect results, focus on making progress. Celebrate the small wins and be kind to yourself if things don't go as planned.

- **Practice:** At the end of each week, reflect on the progress you've made toward your goals. Instead of focusing on what you didn't achieve, celebrate the steps you've taken and adjust your goals if necessary.

Create a Self-Care Plan

As you set goals for the new year, don't forget to include self-care as a priority. Your self-care plan should include daily, weekly, and monthly practices that help you maintain balance, manage stress, and nurture your well-being.

- **Exercise:** Create a self-care plan for the new year by listing three daily, two weekly, and one monthly self-care practice you'll commit to. For example:
  - **Daily:** Drink water, practice gratitude, take a mindful walk
  - **Weekly:** Connect with a friend, do a yoga session
  - **Monthly:** Schedule a massage, take a day off for yourself

Pace Yourself to Avoid Burnout

One of the biggest mistakes people make when setting new year goals is trying to do too much too fast. Burnout can sneak up on you if you're constantly pushing yourself to achieve more. Instead of trying to accomplish everything at once, pace yourself and prioritize rest along the way.

- **Practice:** Break your goals into smaller steps and give yourself time to achieve them. For example, if your goal is to improve your fitness, start with one or two workouts per week and gradually increase as you build momentum. Remember, it's a marathon, not a sprint.

Moving Beyond the Holidays: Embracing Balance and Joy

As the holiday season fades and the new year begins, you have the opportunity to carry forward the lessons you've learned and create a life that feels balanced, joyful, and fulfilling. The mindset of letting go—of perfectionism, unnecessary stress, and obligations—can serve you well beyond the holidays.

By prioritizing self-care, setting realistic goals, and maintaining a mindset of simplicity and ease, you'll be better equipped to navigate life's challenges without sacrificing your well-being. As you move into the new year, remember that balance isn't about doing everything perfectly. It's about making choices that align with your values, support your mental and physical health, and allow you to enjoy the journey.

Conclusion: Letting the Ducks Go

The holiday season often leaves us feeling like we've been juggling too many tasks, trying to please too many people, and managing too much stress. But as we move beyond the holidays and into the new year, we have the chance to *let the ducks go*—to release the stress, the perfectionism, and the unrealistic expectations that weigh us down.

By reflecting on your holiday experience, setting realistic goals for the future, and embracing a mindset of balance and simplicity, you can create a life that feels more aligned with your true values. The practice of letting go isn't just for the holidays—it's a lifelong practice that can bring more peace, joy, and fulfillment to your everyday life.

As you step into the new year, take with you the lessons you've learned, and remember: It's okay to let go of what no longer serves you. By doing so, you make space for the things that truly matter.

Chapter 10

Navigating Difficult Holiday Conversations and Family Strife

*And all your kin and kinsfolk,
That dwell both far and near;
We wish you a Merry Christmas
And a Happy New year*

*Love and joy come to you,
And to you your wassail too;
And God bless you and send you
A Happy New Year
And God send you a Happy New Year.*
(Traditional, n.d.)

Holidays are often seen as a time to come together, celebrate, and reconnect with loved ones. But as many of us know, family gatherings can also bring tension, conflict, and, in some cases, uncomfortable or outright heated conversations. Add in a politically charged climate—especially with major elections on the horizon—and it's common for holiday dinners to devolve into debates or arguments that leave everyone feeling stressed, divided, or upset.

In 2024, as we approach another election year, the chance of political conversations creeping into holiday gatherings is higher than ever. People have strong opinions, and sometimes, without realizing it, those opinions can turn into confrontations that sour the holiday spirit. Whether it's a heated discussion about politics, disagreements about family decisions, or personal conflicts that resurface, it's important to remember that the holiday season is meant to be a time of connection, not division.

This chapter will explore strategies for managing difficult conversations during the holidays, setting boundaries to protect the peace, and keeping the focus on the true purpose of the season—love, connection, and shared experiences. You'll learn how to avoid political meltdowns at the dinner table, navigate family strife with grace, and set expectations for healthy, respectful communication.

The Impact of Political Conversations on Holiday Gatherings

In today's world, political discussions can be highly charged and emotional, especially as elections approach. When these conversations occur at the holiday table, they can quickly lead to frustration, arguments, or even hurt feelings. Political opinions are often deeply personal, tied to our values and beliefs, and when those beliefs are challenged, it's easy for conversations to spiral out of control.

Unfortunately, political conversations can overshadow the joy of the holiday season, turning what should be a time of celebration into a battleground. That's why it's essential to approach these discussions with intention and mindfulness—or avoid them altogether if necessary.

Strategies for Navigating Difficult Conversations

If you find yourself anticipating political or difficult conversations during your holiday gatherings, there are several strategies you can use to steer the focus away from conflict and maintain a peaceful atmosphere. The key is to set boundaries, remain calm, and keep the conversation focused on what matters most during the holidays—connection and togetherness.

Set Boundaries Before the Gathering

One of the most effective ways to prevent political arguments and family conflicts is to set clear boundaries ahead of time. Let your family and friends know that certain topics are off-limits during the holiday celebration, especially if they tend to lead to heated debates or tension.

How to Set Boundaries:

- **Communicate in Advance:** Before the gathering, reach out to your guests and kindly express your wishes. You might say something like, "This year, I'd really love for us to focus on enjoying each other's company and celebrating the holidays. Let's avoid discussing politics and other potentially heated topics."

- **Set the Tone:** At the start of the gathering, gently remind everyone of the boundaries. You could say, "I know we all have strong opinions, but I'd like to ask that we keep politics off the table today so we can focus on the joy of being together."

By establishing these boundaries early on, you set the expectation that the holiday is a time for connection, not conflict.

Deflect With Humor or Grace

Sometimes, even with boundaries in place, difficult conversations can still arise. In these moments, using humor or a graceful redirection can help diffuse the situation before it escalates.

How to Deflect a Heated Conversation:

- **Use Light Humor:** If a political conversation begins to bubble up, you might use light humor to steer the conversation in a different direction. For example, if someone brings up an election-related topic, you could say with a smile, "Ah, we need a holiday truce from politics! Let's save that for another day and focus on dessert instead."

- **Change the Subject:** You can also gently shift the conversation by bringing up a new, noncontroversial topic. "I'd love to hear what everyone's favorite holiday tradition is," or "Has anyone seen any good holiday movies lately?" are simple ways to redirect the focus to something more joyful and inclusive.

The goal is to diffuse tension without escalating the conversation or making anyone feel shut down.

Set Boundaries in the Moment

If a conversation begins to take a difficult turn, and you notice that it's headed toward a political argument or family conflict, don't hesitate to set a boundary in the moment. It's okay to protect the peace of your gathering by gently but firmly steering the conversation away from controversial topics.

How to Set a Boundary in the Moment:

- **Acknowledge and Redirect:** You might say, "I can tell this is something we all feel strongly about, but I'd prefer if we didn't discuss politics today. Let's enjoy the holiday without getting into heavy topics."

- **Empathetic Boundary Setting:** Try to acknowledge the speaker's feelings without diving into the issue. For example, "I understand that this is really important to you, and we can talk about it another time. But for today, let's keep the focus on enjoying each other's company."

Setting boundaries in the moment might feel uncomfortable, but it's necessary for maintaining a peaceful and respectful environment.

Use Active Listening to De-escalate

Sometimes, people just want to feel heard, and acknowledging their feelings can go a long way toward de-escalating a tense conversation. When you find yourself in a difficult conversation, using **active listening** can help you keep the dialogue respectful and calm.

How to Practice Active Listening:

- **Stay Calm:** Even if you disagree, remain calm and composed. Take deep breaths if you feel yourself getting agitated.

- **Acknowledge Their Point of View:** You can say something like, "I hear what you're saying, and I understand this is important to you." This shows that you're listening without necessarily agreeing or engaging in a debate.

- **Steer Back to Neutral Ground:** After acknowledging their perspective, gently steer the conversation back to a lighter, more neutral topic. "I appreciate you sharing your thoughts, but I'd love to hear about your holiday plans."

Active listening can help someone feel respected and heard while still maintaining the peace of the gathering.

Handling Family Strife Beyond Politics

Politics aren't the only source of tension during the holidays. Family conflicts, unresolved issues, and personal disagreements can also resurface, creating an emotionally charged atmosphere. Whether it's a long-standing family dispute or a simple misunderstanding, handling these situations with care and compassion is essential.

Set Expectations for Respectful Communication

Before gathering, it can be helpful to set clear expectations around how you'll handle disagreements or conflicts. Encourage your family to communicate respectfully and avoid bringing up unresolved issues that could create tension during the holidays.

How to Set Communication Expectations:

- **Frame It Around the Holiday:** "Let's make a commitment to keep the holiday focused on love and connection. If any disagreements come up, let's talk about them after the holiday rather than during our celebration."

- **Suggest a Time for Resolution:** If there's an issue that needs to be addressed, offer to discuss it at another time. "I know we need to talk about this, but can we set aside time next week to resolve it instead of doing it today?"

By encouraging respectful communication, you create an atmosphere of understanding and compassion, even if disagreements arise.

Don't Be Afraid to Take a Break

If a conversation becomes too heated or stressful, it's okay to step away. Taking a break allows you to cool down, collect your thoughts, and return to the gathering with a clearer, calmer perspective.

How to Take a Break Gracefully:

- **Excuse Yourself:** If the conversation becomes too overwhelming, you might say, "I need to step outside for a moment to clear my head. I'll be right back."

- **Suggest a Pause:** If the tension is affecting the group, suggest a short break for everyone. "I think we all need a little breather—let's grab some fresh air or refill our drinks and come back to this later."

A break can prevent the conversation from escalating and allow everyone to regain their composure.

Focus on Gratitude and Connection

The holidays are a time to celebrate the people in your life and the love you share. When conversations become difficult or conflicts arise, shifting the focus to gratitude can help everyone remember the true purpose of the season.

How to Bring the Focus Back to Gratitude:

- **Express Appreciation:** When tensions start to build, pause and express gratitude for the people around you. "I'm so thankful we can all be together today, even if we don't always agree. Let's focus on the love we share."

- **Ask Others to Share:** Encourage everyone to take a moment to reflect on what they're grateful for. "Before we move forward, can we each share something we're grateful for this year?"

Gratitude has the power to diffuse tension and bring the conversation back to what matters most: connection, love, and family.

Final Thoughts: Protecting the Peace of the Holidays

Difficult conversations, whether political or personal, can easily disrupt the holiday atmosphere. But with clear boundaries, active listening, and a focus on gratitude and connection, you can navigate these conversations with grace and protect the peace of your holiday gatherings.

As you move into this holiday season, remember that *you have the power to set the tone* for your gatherings. By prioritizing respectful communication, setting healthy boundaries, and keeping the focus on love and togetherness, you can create a holiday experience that's fulfilling and free from unnecessary conflict. Let the holidays be a time of joy, not tension, and embrace the beauty of connection over division.

Chapter 11

Embracing Imperfection: The Beauty of a Messy Holiday

*Jingle bells, jingle bells
Jingle all the way
Oh, what fun it is to ride
In a one-horse open sleigh.*
(Traditional, n.d.)

If you close your eyes and picture the perfect holiday season, what do you see? A meticulously decorated home with twinkling lights in every corner, a table set with perfect place settings, a family gathered around the fireplace with smiles and laughter filling the air? For many of us, this idealized version of the holidays exists only in our minds—or in holiday movies. In reality, the holidays are often far from perfect. The tree might be a little lopsided, the turkey could come out dry, and the gift you ordered might not arrive on time.

And yet, in the midst of these imperfections, there's beauty. A messy holiday, full of imperfections, can still be one of the most meaningful, joyful experiences of the year. In fact, it's often the imperfect moments—the laughter when something goes wrong, the unexpected changes in plans, the flaws in execution—that create the most memorable and fulfilling holidays.

In this last chapter, we'll celebrate the beauty of an imperfect, messy holiday and remind ourselves that the season is not about flawless execution but about connection, love, and shared experiences. We'll share real-life stories of imperfect holidays that turned out to be wonderfully fulfilling and offer final words of encouragement to embrace your version of the holidays, ducks and all.

The Myth of the Perfect Holiday

There's a cultural myth that surrounds the holidays: that in order for the season to be meaningful, everything has to be perfect. From the decorations to the food to the family gatherings, we're often led to believe that there's a "right" way to celebrate and that anything less than perfection is a failure.

But the truth is, this myth sets us up for disappointment and stress. Trying to live up to an unrealistic ideal can leave us feeling anxious, exhausted, and inadequate. The pressure to create a picture-perfect holiday often overshadows the true meaning of the season—connection, love, and gratitude.

In reality, *the most meaningful holidays are rarely perfect*. They're filled with small mistakes, unexpected changes, and messy moments that remind us of our humanity. And that's okay. The beauty of a messy holiday is that it allows us to let go of perfectionism and embrace the joy of simply being present with the people we care about.

The Beauty of Imperfection

When you look back on holidays from years past, what do you remember most? Chances are, it's not the flawless decorations or the perfectly cooked meals. It's the shared laughter, the moments of connection, and the unexpected surprises that made the day memorable.

In fact, some of the most cherished holiday memories often come from moments when things didn't go as planned. Maybe the power went out during a holiday dinner, and you ended up eating by candlelight. Maybe the kids got into a snowball fight that turned the backyard into a muddy mess. Maybe the pie was overcooked, but you laughed about it and ate it anyway.

These imperfect moments are what make the holidays real and meaningful. They remind us that life is messy and unpredictable, and that's where the magic happens.

Real-Life Stories of Messy Holidays

To celebrate the beauty of imperfection, let's look at a few real-life stories of messy holidays that turned out to be wonderfully fulfilling.

The Burnt Turkey and the Best Take-Out Dinner

Wanda always prided herself on hosting a flawless Thanksgiving dinner for her family. She spent days preparing the meal, planning every detail down to the perfect table setting. But one year, disaster struck.

After hours in the oven, the turkey came out burnt—completely inedible.

At first, Wanda t was devastated. She had worked so hard to make everything perfect, and now it seemed like the holiday was ruined. But her family surprised her by laughing off the mishap and suggesting they order takeout instead. They ended up having Chinese food for Thanksgiving, sitting around the table in their pajamas, and laughing about the unexpected turn of events. Wanda realized that her family didn't care about the perfect meal—they just wanted to spend time together. That year's Thanksgiving became one of their most cherished memories.

The Chaotic Christmas Morning

When Vanessa's kids were younger, she always tried to create the perfect Christmas morning—complete with matching pajamas, a beautifully decorated tree, and gifts wrapped in coordinating paper. But one year, everything fell apart. The kids woke up earlier than expected and tore into their presents before Vanessa and her husband had even had a chance to get out of bed. Wrapping paper was everywhere, the tree was knocked over in the excitement, and the family dog decided to chew on a new toy and run through the house, leaving a trail of chaos behind.

At first, Vanessa was overwhelmed by the mess. But then she looked around and saw the pure joy on her kids' faces—their excitement, their laughter, their happiness. She realized that the mess didn't matter. What mattered was that her kids were having the time of their lives, and that they were all together, enjoying the moment. From then on, Vanessa let go of her need for a perfectly orchestrated Christmas and embraced the joy of a messy, chaotic, love-filled morning.

The Forgotten Presents

One holiday season, Mala and Malik had planned a big family gathering, with relatives traveling from out of town. They had organized everything—meals, activities, and even gifts for everyone. But in the chaos of the preparations, they forgot one important detail: They left all the presents at home, a four-hour drive away. When they realized their mistake on Christmas Eve, they panicked.

Instead of focusing on the gifts, the family decided to embrace the situation. They spent Christmas morning playing board games, telling stories, and making homemade gifts out of whatever materials they could find. By the end of the day, everyone agreed that it was one of the best Christmases they had ever had. The absence of presents had allowed them to focus on what truly mattered—spending time together.

Embracing Your Version of the Holidays

The beauty of a messy holiday is that it frees you from the pressure to conform to a perfect ideal. It allows you to create your own version of the holidays—one that reflects your values, your relationships, and your unique circumstances. When you let go of the need for everything to be perfect, you open yourself up to the true meaning of the season.

Focus on Connection, Not Perfection

The holidays are about connection—about spending time with the people you love, creating memories, and sharing experiences. Whether your tree is perfectly decorated, or your dinner is expertly cooked, doesn't really matter. What matters is the feeling of togetherness, the laughter, and the love you share.

- **Practice:** The next time you find yourself stressing over holiday details, pause and ask yourself, "Does this really matter? What's more important—getting everything perfect or enjoying time with my loved ones?"

Let Go of Expectations

One of the biggest sources of holiday stress is the expectations we place on ourselves—expectations to create the perfect experience, meet everyone's needs, and manage every detail flawlessly. But when you let go of those expectations, you create space for spontaneity, joy, and imperfection.

- **Practice:** Before the holidays begin, take a moment to reflect on your expectations. What can you let go of? What's enormously important to you? By releasing unrealistic expectations, you'll find that you enjoy the holidays more and feel less pressure to live up to an impossible standard.

Celebrate the Messy Moments

When things go wrong during the holidays—and they will—try to see the humor and beauty in the mess. These are the moments that become stories, that bond you with your loved ones, and that make the holidays memorable.

- **Practice:** The next time something doesn't go as planned, instead of getting upset, take a deep breath, and remind yourself that this is part of the magic of the holidays. Imperfection is what makes these moments real.

Embrace Your Own Traditions

The holidays don't have to look like everyone else's to be meaningful. Whether you celebrate with big family gatherings or quiet evenings at home, elaborate meals or takeout dinners, matching pajamas or no pajamas at all—your holiday is yours to create. Embrace the traditions that matter to you and let go of the ones that don't.

- **Practice:** Reflect on what traditions truly bring you joy and focus on those. Let go of any traditions that feel like obligations or that don't align with your values. Remember, the holidays are about celebrating in a way that feels authentic to you.

Final Words of Encouragement: Ducks and All

As we conclude this journey through the holiday season, remember that the holidays are meant to be enjoyed, not perfected. Life is messy, unpredictable, and full of surprises—and that's what makes it beautiful. The small stressors—the ducks that peck away at your peace—will always be there. But when you choose to embrace imperfection, to let go of the need for control, and to focus on what truly matters, you create a holiday season filled with meaning, connection, and joy.

So this year, give yourself permission to have a messy holiday. Let the ducks waddle by, laugh at the burned turkey, and celebrate the beauty of imperfection. The moments that don't go as planned are often the ones you'll cherish the most. And in the end, it's not about the perfect decorations, the perfect gifts, or the perfect meal—it's about the love, laughter, and memories you create along the way.

Here's to a beautifully imperfect holiday, ducks and all.

Conclusion

Flying Free from the Holiday Flock

> *Therefore, Christian men, be sure,*
> *while God's gifts possessing,*
> *You who now will bless the poor*
> *shall yourselves find blessing.*
> **Good King Wenceslas (Neale, 1853)**

As we come to the end of our journey together, I hope this book has offered you new ways to think about the holiday season. We've explored how easy it is to get caught up in the stress and perfectionism of the holidays, and how quickly small tasks—the ducks that never seem to stop quacking—can overwhelm our sense of peace and joy. But as we've learned, there's a different way to approach the holidays, one that centers on balance, self-care, and what truly matters: connection, love, and shared experiences.

This conclusion isn't just about closing one holiday chapter—it's about creating a legacy. *Remember, you're not only shaping your own experience of the holidays, but you're also setting the tone for the next generation.* Your children, nieces, nephews, grandchildren, and even younger colleagues are watching how you handle the season, learning from your approach. They'll see whether the holidays are a time of joy and connection—or whether they're marked by stress, overwhelm, and burnout.

The traditions you establish now can influence how future generations experience the holidays. If you prioritize balance, joy, and self-care, you're teaching them that the holidays can be a time of warmth and connection, rather than a race to meet unrealistic expectations. By letting go of perfectionism and embracing the beauty of imperfection, you model a sustainable and sane approach to the holidays—one that will stand the test of time.

Key Messages: Focus on What Truly Matters

Throughout this book, we've highlighted a key message: *The holidays are about what truly matters, not about the perfect execution of tasks or traditions*. They're about love, connection, and creating memories that last. Let's take a moment to revisit the core lessons we've explored together.

Let Go of Perfectionism

Perfectionism is one of the greatest sources of holiday stress. The pressure to create a flawless holiday experience can lead to anxiety, exhaustion, and feelings of inadequacy. But as we've learned, the beauty of the holidays lies in their imperfections. The burned cookies, the last-minute changes, and the messy moments often turn into the memories we cherish most.

Takeaway: Let go of the need for perfection and focus on what matters. Your loved ones won't remember whether the table settings were flawless—they'll remember the laughter, the connection, and the love they felt.

Prioritize Connection Over Tasks

During the holidays, it's easy to get caught up in the endless to-do lists—shopping, cooking, decorating, and attending events. But when we focus too much on tasks, we lose sight of the deeper purpose of the season: connection with the people we care about.

Takeaway: Prioritize time spent with family and friends over completing every task on your list. The holidays are about being present with the people who matter most. Let go of the trivial details and embrace the moments of joy and togetherness.

Create Balance Through Boundaries

A balanced holiday season is one where your energy is spent on what brings you fulfillment, not on fulfilling every obligation. Setting boundaries—whether it's saying no to a party or scaling back on gift-giving—helps you protect your peace and avoid burnout.

Takeaway: Boundaries are essential for a healthy holiday season. Decide what's most important to you and let go of the rest. By creating balance, you'll have the energy to enjoy the moments that truly matter.

Prioritize Self-Care Without Guilt

Self-care during the holidays isn't selfish—it's necessary. When you take care of yourself, you're able to approach the season with more energy, patience, and joy. And remember, when younger generations see you prioritizing self-care, they learn that it's not only acceptable but essential.

Takeaway: Make self-care part of your holiday routine and do so without guilt. Whether it's taking time for a walk, practicing mindfulness, or simply resting when you need it, self-care is what enables you to show up fully for the people you love.

Embrace Imperfection as a Family Tradition

It's important to acknowledge that the way we handle holiday stress doesn't just impact us—it sets the tone for future generations. Children, nieces, nephews, and grandchildren learn about the holidays by watching how we celebrate. If they see us stressed, overwhelmed, and focused on perfection, that's what they'll come to associate with the holiday season. But if they see us embracing imperfection, prioritizing connection, and setting boundaries, they'll learn that the holidays can be joyful and fulfilling.

Takeaway: Embrace imperfection as a family tradition. Let your children see that it's okay if the cookies burn, if plans change, or if things don't go perfectly. What matters is the love and laughter shared. By modeling this mindset, you're teaching the next generation to approach the holidays with a healthy, balanced perspective.

Setting Healthy, Sustainable Traditions

As you prepare for future holidays, remember that the traditions you establish now will influence how your family celebrates for years to come. Be mindful of the lessons you're passing down. Instead of teaching younger generations that the holidays are about stress, perfectionism, and exhaustion, show them that the holidays can be a time of joy, balance, and meaningful connection.

Start Simple Traditions

Not every tradition needs to be grand or elaborate. Some of the most meaningful traditions are the simplest—baking cookies together, watching a favorite holiday movie, or taking a family walk in the snow. These moments of connection are what your family will remember, not the perfect meal or the flawless decorations.

- **Practice:** Focus on creating simple, sustainable traditions that emphasize connection over perfection. These are the traditions that will stand the test of time.

Teach the Importance of Self-Care

One of the most valuable lessons you can pass down to younger generations is the importance of self-care, especially during the holidays. Teach them that it's okay to take breaks, to say no when necessary, and to prioritize their well-being.

- **Practice:** Involve your children in self-care practices during the holidays. This could be as simple as setting aside time for quiet reflection, going for a walk as a family, or practicing gratitude together.

Model Healthy Boundaries

Younger generations learn by example. If they see you setting healthy boundaries—saying no to unnecessary obligations, simplifying your holiday routine, and taking time for self-care—they'll learn that it's okay to protect their peace, too.

- **Practice:** Be open about the boundaries you're setting during the holidays. Explain to your children or loved ones why you're choosing to prioritize certain activities and let go of others. This helps normalize the practice of setting boundaries.

A Final Call: Letting Go of the Ducks for Good

As we conclude this book, I want to leave you with a final message: *Let go of the holiday ducks and reclaim your peace*. You don't have to chase every task, meet every expectation, or create the perfect holiday experience. The true beauty of the holidays lies in the messy, imperfect moments—moments of connection, laughter, and love.

Remember, the way you approach the holidays influences not only your own experience but the experience of future generations. By embracing balance, self-care, and imperfection, you're creating a legacy of joy and connection that will last for years to come.

So, this holiday season, and every season that follows, give yourself permission to let go. Fly free from the holiday flock, set healthy, sustainable traditions, and focus on what truly matters. When you do, you'll find that the holidays—and life—become much more joyful, peaceful, and meaningful.

Here's to a holiday season filled with love, laughter, and the beauty of imperfection.

About the Author

Rochelle Brandon, MD, is a seasoned gynecologist with extensive experience counseling women about the stresses of life's nonessential distractions. Having faced her own struggles with the overwhelming minutiae that can consume daily life, Dr. Brandon combines her firsthand experiences with professional insights to address the common, yet often overlooked, challenges that many women face.

In *Pecked to Death by Ducks: How Minutiae Can Distract You From Living Your Best Life*, she shared practical advice and compassionate guidance, offering readers a roadmap to reclaim their focus and well-being amid the chaos of modern life.

Now, Dr. Brandon tackles the distractions of the holidays in *Six Geese A-Laying: The Never-Ending Holiday Ducks.*

Find out more at www.RochelleBrandon.com

Appendix

The holiday season can feel overwhelming with tasks to complete, events to attend, and people to please. However, with a bit of planning and intention, you can create a holiday experience that's meaningful, balanced, and joyful. The following worksheets and exercises are designed to help you prioritize what matters most, set boundaries, and integrate mindfulness and self-care into your holiday routine. You'll also find a list of recommended reading to deepen your journey toward a more peaceful and fulfilling holiday season.

Worksheet 1: Prioritizing Holiday Tasks

Use this worksheet to sort your holiday tasks by importance, identifying what truly matters and what can be simplified or eliminated.

Step 1: List Your Holiday Tasks

Write down everything you think you need to do for the holiday season.

1. _____

2. _____

3. _____

4. _____

5. _____

6. _____

7. _____

8. _____

Step 2: Categorize Your Tasks

Sort each task into one of three categories:

- **Must-Do:** Tasks that are non-negotiable, either because they're essential to your holiday or because they're required.

- **Nice-to-Do:** Tasks that would be nice to accomplish but aren't critical to your enjoyment of the holiday

- **Let Go:** Tasks that are not necessary and can be simplified, delegated, or eliminated altogether

Example:

- **Must-Do:** Buying gifts for immediate family

- **Nice-to-Do:** Sending out holiday cards

- **Let Go:** Baking five different kinds of holiday cookies

Step 3: Plan Accordingly

Focus your energy on the **Must-Do** items and decide which **Nice-to-Do** tasks you can incorporate without adding stress. Give yourself permission to let go of tasks that don't truly serve you.

Worksheet 2: Setting Boundaries for the Holidays

Setting boundaries can protect your time, energy, and mental health. Use this worksheet to clarify your boundaries for the holiday season.

Step 1: Identify Areas Where Boundaries Are Needed

Consider the areas where you feel overwhelmed during the holidays. This might include

- attending too many social events.
- hosting gatherings.
- gift-giving expectations.
- family dynamics.

Write down the areas where you need to set boundaries:

1. _____
2. _____
3. _____

Step 2: Define Your Boundaries

For each area, write a clear, realistic boundary that protects your energy and well-being.

Example:

- **Social Events:** "I will only attend two holiday parties this season and will graciously decline any others."
- **Family Dynamics:** "I will leave family gatherings by 8:00 p.m. to ensure I have time to rest."

- **Gift-Giving:** "I will set a gift budget and stick to it, choosing thoughtful but simple gifts."

Step 3: Communicate Your Boundaries

Once you've defined your boundaries, think about how you'll communicate them to others. Write down any scripts or phrases you might use.

Example:

- "Thank you so much for the invitation, but I've decided to keep my schedule light this year. I hope you have a wonderful holiday!"

Communicating your boundaries with kindness and clarity will help you protect your time and energy while maintaining healthy relationships.

Worksheet 3: Reflecting on What Matters Most

Reflect on your values and intentions for the holiday season to focus on what truly brings you joy and meaning.

Step 1: What Do You Want to Feel?

Write down how you want to feel during the holiday season. Examples might include "peaceful," "connected," "joyful," or "grateful."

- _____
- _____
- _____

Step 2: What Are Your Priorities?

Think about the activities, traditions, or experiences that are most important to you. These are the things you should prioritize to align your holiday with your values.

- _____
- _____
- _____

Step 3: Letting Go of What Doesn't Matter

What holiday tasks, traditions, or obligations don't align with how you want to feel? What can you let go of or simplify?

- _____
- _____
- _____

By reflecting on your priorities and letting go of the rest, you'll create a more meaningful and fulfilling holiday season.

Mindfulness and Self-Care Exercises for the Holidays

Integrating mindfulness and self-care into your holiday routine can help reduce stress and keep you grounded. Try these simple practices to nurture your well-being.

Holiday Gratitude Practice

Each morning, take a few moments to reflect on three things you're grateful for during the holiday season. This practice shifts your focus from stress to appreciation.

- Example: "I'm grateful for the chance to spend time with my family," or "I'm grateful for the beauty of the winter season."

Deep Breathing Exercise

When you feel overwhelmed, pause, and take three deep breaths. Focus on your breath as it moves in and out of your body, letting go of any tension with each exhale.

1. **Inhale:** Breathe in slowly through your nose, counting to four.
2. **Hold:** Hold your breath for a count of four.
3. **Exhale:** Exhale slowly through your mouth, counting to four.
4. Repeat as needed.

Mindful Walking

Take a short walk outside and pay attention to your surroundings—the sounds, smells, and sensations. This simple exercise helps you reconnect with the present moment and creates a sense of calm during busy holiday days.

Digital Detox

For one hour each evening, step away from your devices—no emails, no social media, no online shopping. Use this time to relax, connect with loved ones, or enjoy a quiet activity like reading or journaling.

Evening Wind-Down

Create a calming evening routine that helps you unwind after a busy day. This might include dimming the lights, enjoying a cup of tea, or practicing a few gentle stretches before bed.

By using these worksheets and exercises and diving into further reading, you'll be well-equipped to embrace a holiday season that's filled with balance, joy, and peace. Remember, the holidays are yours to shape—so focus on what truly matters, let go of the rest, and take care of yourself along the way.

Recommended Reading

To deepen your exploration of mindfulness, self-care, and simplifying the holidays, here are some books that offer valuable insights and practical advice.

The Gifts of Imperfection by Brené Brown

A powerful guide to embracing vulnerability and letting go of the need for perfection, this book offers wisdom for navigating the messiness of life with compassion and self-acceptance.

The Joy of Less by Francine Jay

A practical guide to simplifying your life, this book encourages readers to let go of unnecessary clutter—both physical and emotional—and focus on what truly brings joy and fulfillment.

Essentialism: The Disciplined Pursuit of Less by Greg McKeown

This book is all about focusing on what matters most and eliminating distractions. It's a great read for anyone looking to simplify their life and create more meaning during the holidays and beyond.

The Art of Simple Living by Shunmyo Masuno

Written by a Zen Buddhist monk, this book offers 100 daily practices for finding peace, joy, and simplicity in everyday life.

Present Over Perfect by Shauna Niequist

In this reflective memoir, Niequist explores the importance of slowing down, letting go of perfectionism, and finding joy in being present for life's most meaningful moments.

Full Catastrophe Living: Using the Wisdom of Your Body and Mind to Face Stress, Pain, and Illness (2013 revised ed.) by Jon Kabat-Zinn

Through mindful meditation techniques, the book teaches readers how to cultivate awareness and resilience in the face of life's challenges. Kabat-Zinn's insights provide a holistic approach to healing and well-being, making it an essential resource for those seeking balance and inner peace.

References

Guendelman, S., Medeiros, S., & Rampes, H. (2017). Mindfulness and emotion regulation: Insights from neurobiological, psychological, and clinical studies. *Frontiers in Psychology, 8*, 220. https://doi.org/10.3389/fpsyg.2017.00220

Hofmann, S. G., Sawyer, A. T., Witt, A. A., & Oh, D. (2010). The effect of mindfulness-based therapy on anxiety and depression: A meta-analytic review. *Journal of Consulting and Clinical Psychology, 78*(2), 169–183. https://doi.org/10.1037/a0018555

Hölzel, B. K., Lazar, S. W., Gard, T., Schuman-Olivier, Z., Vago, D. R., & Ott, U. (2011). How does mindfulness meditation work? Proposing mechanisms of action from a conceptual and neural perspective. *Perspectives on Psychological Science, 6*(6), 537–559. https://doi.org/10.1177/1745691611419671

Jha, A. P., Krompinger, J., & Baime, M. J. (2007). Mindfulness training modifies subsystems of attention. *Cognitive, Affective, & Behavioral Neuroscience, 7*(2), 109–119. https://doi.org/10.3758/CABN.7.2.109

Kabat-Zinn, J. (2013). *Full catastrophe living: Using the wisdom of your body and mind to face stress, pain, and illness* (Revised ed.). Bantam Books.

Song References

Bach, J. S. (1723). *Jesu, joy of man's desiring* [Song].

Brackett, J. (1848). *Simple gifts* [Song].

Longfellow, H. W. (1863). *I heard the bells on Christmas day* [Song].

Mohr, J., & Gruber, F. X. (1818). *Silent night, holy night* [Song].

Traditional. (1885). *Christmas is coming, the goose is getting fat* [Song].

Traditional. (n.d.). *Deck the halls* [Song].

Traditional. (n.d.). *Go tell it on the mountain* [Song].

Neale, J. M. (1853). *Good King Wenceslas* [Song].

Traditional. (n.d.). *Here we come a-wassailing* [Song].

Traditional. (n.d.). *I saw three ships* [Song].

Sears, E. H. (1849). *It came upon the midnight clear* [Song].

Traditional. (n.d.). *Jingle bells* [Song].

Traditional. (n.d.). *The twelve days of Christmas* [Song].

Thank you for supporting an independent author and publisher.

If you enjoyed this book, please leave a review on Amazon.com.

If you find this book helpful, please recommend it to friends.

Thank you,

Rochelle Brandon, MD

Lipsey & Love Legacy Press

Printed in Great Britain
by Amazon